Gourmet's
Casual Entertaining

EASY YEAR-ROUND MENUS FOR FAMILY AND FRIENDS

FROM THE EDITORS OF
Gourmet

CONDÉ NAST BOOKS
RANDOM HOUSE
NEW YORK

Copyright © 2001

The Condé Nast Publications Inc. All rights reserved under International and Pan-American Copyright Conventions. Published in the United States by Random House, Inc., New York, and simultaneously in Canada by Random House of Canada Limited, Toronto.

LIBRARY OF CONGRESS
CATALOGING-IN-PUBLICATION DATA

GOURMET'S CASUAL ENTERTAINING:
Easy year-round menus for family and friends
From the editors of Gourmet

        p. cm.

Includes index

ISBN 0-375-50735-3

1. Cookery.   2. Entertaining.   I. Gourmet

TX714.G6813 2001

642'.4—dc21   2001019781

Random House website address: www.atrandom.com

Some of the recipes in this work were published previously in Gourmet magazine.

Printed in the United States of America on acid-free paper.

98765432
FIRST EDITION

Informative text in this book was written by Diane Keitt, Ellen Morrissey, Jane Daniels Lear, and Kemp Miles Minifie.

The text of this book was set in Seria by Bill SMITH STUDIO. The four-color separations were done by American Color, Applied Graphic Technologies, and Quad/Graphics, Inc. The book was printed and bound at R. R. Donnelley and Sons. Stock is Sterling Ultra Web Gloss, Westvāco.

FOR CONDÉ NAST BOOKS

Lisa Faith Phillips, Vice President/General Manager
Tom Downing, Direct Marketing Director
Deborah Williams, Associate Operations Director
Peter Immediato, Business Manager
Catherine Punch, Direct Marketing Manager
Jennifer Zalewski, Direct Marketing Associate
Eric Levy, Inventory Assistant
Barbara Giordano, Direct Marketing Assistant
Alicia Hodroski, Direct Marketing Assistant
Richard B. Elman, Production Manager

FOR GOURMET BOOKS

Diane Keitt, Director
Ellen Morrissey, Associate Editor

FOR GOURMET MAGAZINE

Ruth Reichl, Editor in Chief
Zanne Early Stewart, Executive Food Editor
Kemp Miles Minifie, Senior Food Editor
Alexis M. Touchet, Associate Food Editor
Lori Walther Powell, Food Editor
Katy Massam, Food Editor
Shelton Wiseman, Food Editor
Ruth Cousineau, Food Editor
Gina Marie Miraglia, Food Editor
Romulo A. Yanes, Photographer

Produced in association with JaBS MEDIA
Jacqueline A. Ball, Publisher
Anne B. Wright, Project Editor
Jeffrey Rutzky, Production Manager
Marilyn Flaig, Indexer

VERTIGO DESIGN, NYC
Jacket and Book Design

Front Jacket: Apricot-stuffed pork loin (page 97); Baby spinach and mint salad (page 98); Parsnip-potato mash (page 98).

Back Jacket: Leek and potato keftédes (page 104); Pesto cheese straws (page 70); Cranberry-lime cooler (page 101); Piquillo pepper mousse with pita chips (page 96).

IT'S AMAZING how much time and energy is takes to put together a book that encourages the reader to spend a minimum of both. Though we set out to promote the idea of *casual* entertaining, we adhered to a schedule that was anything but easy or carefree, and everyone involved stuck to it with fierce determination. The following *Gourmet* food editors developed outstanding new recipes: Alexis Touchet (easy Saturday nights), Lori Powell (lazy Sundays), Ruth Cousineau (casual celebrations, including the menu shown on the front jacket), Gina Miraglia (grills), and Tracey Seaman (picnics). Melissa Roberts stepped in to cross-test many of the recipes. Zanne Stewart, Executive Food Editor, and Kemp Minifie, Senior Food Editor, consulted on each menu and tasted new recipes, and Gerald Asher, *Gourmet's* Wine Editor, offered wine suggestions where appropriate.

While we were scouting locations to shoot new photography, Joe Bianco and Liz Powell graciously allowed us to use their gorgeous home. *Gourmet* photographer Romulo Yanes captured the warm spirit of the book perfectly on the front jacket, with prop styling by Jeannie Oberholtzer and food styling by Melissa Roberts, and on the back jacket with food styling by Lori Powell. Ellen Morrissey and Ian Knauer posed for the front jacket; Caryn Levitt, Richard Pellicci, and Lisa Phillips modeled for the back jacket photo. Romulo also shot most of the photographs that appear throughout; other photography was provided by Melanie Acevedo, Quentin Bacon, Antoine Bootz, Jean Cazals, Miki Duisterhof, Dana Gallagher, Lisa Hubbard, Elisabeth Hughes, John Kernick, Rick Lew, Rita Maas, Maura McEvoy, Minh + Wass, Victoria Pearson, Dan Peebles, Nick Pope, Alan Richardson, Ellen Silverman, Jonelle Weaver, and Anna Williams.

Cheryl Brown and Kathleen Duffy Freud offered keen editorial input, and Jane Daniels Lear and Kemp Minifie kindly granted permission to use their informative "boxes" throughout. We would also like to acknowledge Jeffrey Rutzky and Anne Wright of JaBS MEDIA and Richard Elman of Random House for their production assistance, with special thanks to Anne for her meticulous attention to every little detail. This is our first book with the talented team at Vertigo Design, and we'd like to thank Alison Lew and Renata de Oliveira for translating our ideas into a book that's ultimately as beautiful and engaging as the most memorable get-togethers with friends.

Contents

"LET'S GET TOGETHER SOON." How often do we say this and then wonder how we can manage it, and when? It's no wonder that the restaurant business is booming—with a few quick calls, plans and reservations are made and that's that. Of course, we might worry about the food and the ambiance and whether everyone will be pleased, but sharing a meal with those we care about is really what's important.

But let's be honest—a relaxed meal at home with family and friends is so much better than a restaurant experience can ever be. And so, with the help of Gourmet's food editors, we set out to create a cookbook that would inspire even the most harried among us to entertain casually at home. We talked about great informal meals that we personally had enjoyed over the years. Favorites often took place away from the dining room—on a porch, at the lake, in front of a fire—and invariably they occurred on a weekend or when we were on vacation in the country or at the beach, when time was not so rushed. Picnics and barbecues were repeatedly mentioned, as were celebrations, like a memorable 40th birthday party and an all-day graduation party. All captured that "feel good" sentiment we were trying to replicate. We decided to pool our experiences and to improve upon them.

We also talked at length about what's important (the food, the setting, making everyone feel comfortable) and what's not (polished silverware, fancy centerpieces, and fussy presentations). The goal, we concluded, was to keep everything—the food, the look, the setting—as simple as possible. If we could develop supereasy seasonal recipes with readily available ingredients (no mail order to speak of) and offer plenty of dishes that can be made ahead of time, we'd have the winning formula for our book.

Eight months of planning and cooking and editing later, we present 32 new menus for entertaining casually and simply, yet with great style. Remember, getting together with family and friends is what it's all about. And if the chicken slides off the platter or the dog eats dessert, just open another bottle of wine and savor the moment. This is an occasion that will never be forgotten.

THE EDITORS OF GOURMET BOOKS

SATURDAY NIGHT is the
obvious choice for entertaining—it falls smack in the
middle of the weekend, sur-
rounded by the greatest
amount of free time you're
likely to have all week. But
who wants to spend an entire
day preparing for company,
only to spend the next day
exhausted and wiped out?
That's why we created seven
menus that are carefree
and easygoing for every-
one involved.

Easy saturday nights

Dinner on the porch

IT'S LATE SUMMERTIME, and the living couldn't get much easier. Pick a few vegetables and herbs from the garden (or farmers market, the next best thing) and call a few friends over for dinner al fresco. The soup, the eggplant purée for the bruschetta, even dessert—a deceptively simple ice cream and cookie stack laced with rum and topped with a heady caramel sauce—can be made in the morning, all in ridiculously little time. Go ahead, take the afternoon off. Tonight, you'll toss the pasta on the spot with ripe cherry tomatoes, fresh basil, and creamy goat cheese. Afterwards, your friends will want to linger. If only summer could last forever....

Eggplant bruschetta

1¼ lb eggplant, halved lengthwise

1 teaspoon coriander seeds, toasted and cooled

1 small garlic clove, minced

¼ cup finely chopped fresh flat-leaf parsley

3 tablespoons extra-virgin olive oil

½ teaspoon fresh lemon juice

6 (⅓-inch-thick) diagonal slices Italian bread, toasted

Preheat oven to 375°F.

Put eggplant, cut sides down, on a well-oiled shallow baking pan. Bake in middle of oven until very soft, about 1 hour, then cool.

Finely grind coriander seeds in a coffee/spice grinder or with a mortar and pestle.

Scoop eggplant flesh into a food processor, discarding skin, then purée with ground coriander, garlic, parsley, oil, lemon juice, and salt and pepper to taste.

Spread 1 tablespoon purée on each toast.

COOKS' NOTE

• Eggplant purée may be made 1 day ahead and chilled, covered.

SERVES 6

Chilled yellow bell pepper and thyme soup

4 yellow bell peppers (1½ lb), chopped

1 onion, chopped

1 large garlic clove, chopped

2 tablespoons olive oil

1 (14½-oz) can chicken broth

2 cups water

1 tablespoon fresh thyme

1 small bay leaf (not California)

Garnish: small thyme sprigs

Cook bell peppers, onion, and garlic in oil in a 3-quart heavy saucepan over moderately low heat, covered, stirring occasionally, until vegetables are softened but not browned, 8 to 10 minutes.

Add broth, water, thyme, and bay leaf and simmer, uncovered, until peppers are very tender, 18 to 20 minutes.

Discard bay leaf and purée soup in batches in a blender, transferring to a metal bowl (use caution when blending hot liquids). Cool soup, uncovered, then chill, covered, until cold, about 3 hours.

COOKS' NOTE

• Soup may be made 1 day ahead and chilled, covered.

MAKES ABOUT 5½ CUPS

Pasta with tomatoes and goat cheese

1 lb gemelli or penne

2¾ lb cherry tomatoes, halved

5 to 6 oz soft mild goat cheese, crumbled

⅔ cup coarsely chopped Kalamata
or other brine-cured black olives

¾ cup torn fresh basil

Cook pasta in a 6-quart pot of boiling salted water until just al dente, then drain.

While pasta cooks, toss tomatoes with salt to taste in a bowl.

Toss hot pasta with goat cheese in a large bowl until cheese is melted and coats pasta. Add tomatoes with juices that have accumulated in bowl, olives, basil, and salt and pepper to taste, then toss to combine.

COOKS' NOTES

• To prevent basil leaves from discoloring, don't tear them until just before pasta is done.

• It's a good idea to taste your goat cheese before using it (or before buying it, if possible). One of the soft goat cheeses we tried seemed a bit too strong for this dish.

SERVES 6

Move over cherry tomatoes...

ALTHOUGH OUR PASTA dish calls for cherry tomatoes, feel free to substitute the trendy little "grape" tomato that we are seeing everywhere these days (see photo, right). It is actually a new hybrid named "Santa," developed by a seed company in Taiwan. The tomatoes grow in long clusters, hence their "grape" nickname. Here's where the story gets complicated: Only that one seed company can produce true Santa seed, so seed is scarce. But some growers are raising faux Santas. Does it matter to cooks? All of the grape tomatoes we've tried have a complex, remarkably good tomato flavor.

— JANE DANIELS LEAR

Coffee ice cream chocolate stack with caramel sauce

60 chocolate wafer cookies (two 9-oz packages)

¼ cup plus 1 tablespoon dark rum

3 pints superpremium coffee ice cream, softened

¾ cup sugar

¼ cup water

¾ cup heavy cream

2 tablespoons unsalted butter

Special equipment: an 8- by 2-inch square metal baking pan

MAKE STACK:

Lightly oil bottom and sides of baking pan and line with a 2-foot piece of plastic wrap, letting excess hang over sides.

Working quickly, lightly brush 20 cookies on 1 side with some of ¼ cup rum, then arrange in 1 layer in bottom of pan, overlapping slightly to fit snugly. Beat half of ice cream with an electric mixer until smooth and spread evenly over cookies. Brush 20 more cookies with some more rum and beat remaining half of ice cream. Make another layer in same manner. Brush remaining cookies with remainder of ¼ cup rum and layer evenly over ice cream. Fold plastic wrap over top of stack and freeze until solid, about 6 hours.

MAKE SAUCE:

Cook sugar in a 2- to 3-quart dry heavy saucepan over moderately low heat, stirring slowly with a fork, until melted and pale golden. Cook caramel, without stirring, swirling pan, until deep golden. Remove pan from heat and carefully pour water down side of pan in a slow stream (mixture will vigorously steam and caramel will harden). Re-

turn to heat and simmer, stirring, until caramel is dissolved and mixture is thickened, 1 to 2 minutes. Stir in cream and remaining tablespoon rum and simmer, stirring occasionally, 1 minute. Stir in butter and a pinch of salt and cook, stirring, until butter is melted.

Soften stack slightly and cut into 9 squares. Serve with warm sauce spooned over each square.

COOKS' NOTES

• Stack may be made 3 days ahead. Frozen stack may be cut into squares, wrapped individually in plastic wrap, and kept frozen in a large resealable plastic bag.

• Caramel sauce may be made 3 days ahead and chilled, covered.

MAKES **9** SQUARES

Come for cocktails

COCKTAIL TRENDS may come and go, but cocktail parties live on. They're inherently festive, and somehow less daunting than all but the simplest dinner parties. A couple of hours of drinks, hors d'oeuvres, and a little lively conversation, then your guests are on their merry way. (Just be sure to establish a firm time frame in advance, so no one expects dinner.) Mix up some punch and the iced tea, set out your snacks, and kick back. Easy does it, indeed.

Tabbouleh-stuffed grape leaves

1 (1-lb) jar brine-packed Greek
or California grape leaves

⅓ cup bulgur

1½ cups fresh flat-leaf parsley,
finely chopped

1 cup fresh mint, finely chopped

¼ cup finely chopped red onion

¼ cup dried currants

4½ tablespoons olive oil

3 tablespoons fresh lemon juice

About 1⅔ cups vegetable or chicken broth

Unfurl stacks of grape leaves in a large bowl of water (leaves should remain stacked) and gently agitate without separating leaves. Blanch stacks in a large pot of boiling water 3 minutes, then drain in a colander. Rinse stacks under cold water and drain well. Reserve 6 leaves for lining pan and set aside 24 untorn leaves, each measuring about 5½ inches wide.

Soak bulgur in boiling-hot water to cover by 1 inch for 15 minutes, then drain in a sieve, pressing hard to extract as much water as possible. Toss together bulgur, parsley, mint, onion, currants, 2 tablespoons oil, 1½ tablespoons lemon juice, and salt and pepper to taste.

Arrange 1 untorn grape leaf, smooth side down, on a kitchen towel. Trim stem flush with leaf (if leaf is very large, trim to 5½ inches wide), saving any trimmings. Spoon 1 rounded tablespoon filling onto leaf near stem end, then tightly roll up filling in leaf, folding in sides and squeezing roll to pack filling. (Roll should be about 3½ inches long.) Make 23 more rolls in same manner.

Line bottom of a 2½-quart heavy saucepan with leaf trimmings and 6 reserved leaves. Arrange rolls, seam sides down, close together in layers over leaves, seasoning each layer with salt. Drizzle with 1½ tablespoons oil and remaining 1½ tablespoons lemon juice, then cover with an inverted heatproof plate slightly smaller than pan, pressing down gently. Add just enough broth to reach rim of plate and bring to a boil. Cook rolls at a bare simmer, covered with plate and lid, until leaves are tender and most of liquid is absorbed, 45 to 50 minutes.

Remove from heat and transfer rolls with tongs to a platter to cool, brushing with remaining tablespoon oil. Serve warm or cold.

COOKS' NOTE

• Stuffed grape leaves may be made 3 days ahead and chilled in an airtight container.

MAKES 24 HORS D'OEUVRES

Chicken satés with peanut curry sauce

3 cups well-stirred canned unsweetened coconut milk

2 tablespoons soy sauce

1 tablespoon curry powder

1½ teaspoons ground coriander seeds

4 teaspoons cornstarch

2 (1½-lb) whole skinless boneless chicken breasts, each cut lengthwise into 10 strips (½-inch-thick)

1½ cups salted dry-roasted peanuts, finely ground

2 teaspoons fresh lime juice

¼ teaspoon dried hot red pepper flakes, or to taste

2 teaspoons minced fresh cilantro

Special equipment: 20 (8-inch) bamboo skewers, soaked in water 30 minutes

Stir together coconut milk, soy sauce, curry powder, and ground coriander. Transfer 1 cup to a bowl and stir in cornstarch. Reserve remaining coconut mixture, covered and chilled.

Add chicken to cornstarch mixture, stirring to coat, then marinate, covered and chilled, at least 1 hour.

Prepare grill for cooking.

Simmer reserved coconut mixture, peanuts, lime juice, and red pepper flakes in a small saucepan, stirring occasionally, until thickened, about 10 minutes. Transfer dipping sauce to a small bowl and cool.

Thread 1 piece chicken onto each skewer, then grill on an oiled rack set 5 to 6 inches over glowing coals until cooked through, about 3 minutes on each side.

Sprinkle dipping sauce with cilantro and serve at room temperature with satés.

COOKS' NOTE
• Chicken strips can marinate up to 1 day.

MAKES 20 SATÉS

Shrimp satés with greek garlic sauce

10 large garlic cloves

48 medium shrimp (1½ lb), deveined and shelled, leaving tails intact

3 tablespoons chopped fresh rosemary

¾ cup plus 3 tablespoons extra-virgin olive oil

8 slices firm white sandwich bread, crusts discarded and bread torn into pieces

⅓ cup sliced blanched almonds, finely ground

9 tablespoons fresh lemon juice

Special equipment: 24 (8-inch) bamboo skewers, soaked in water 1 hour

Coarsely chop 3 garlic cloves and stir together with shrimp, rosemary, and 3 tablespoons oil. Marinate shrimp, covered and chilled, at least 1 hour.

Prepare grill for cooking.

Soak bread in ¾ cup water 15 minutes, then squeeze out excess water.

Finely chop remaining 7 garlic cloves and purée with bread and almonds in a food processor until fluffy and very smooth. With motor running, add remaining ¾ cup oil in a slow stream, blending until emulsified, then blend in lemon juice and salt to taste. Transfer dipping sauce to a small bowl.

Thread 2 shrimp onto each skewer, then grill on an oiled rack set 5 to 6 inches over glowing coals until just cooked through, about 1 minute on each side.

Serve satés with garlic dipping sauce at room temperature.

COOKS' NOTE

• Shrimp can marinate up to 1 day.

MAKES **24** SATÉS

Smoked salmon and pickled cucumber on rye

½ cup cider vinegar

½ cup water

6 tablespoons sugar

½ small English cucumber, halved lengthwise and cut crosswise into 1/16-inch-thick slices

1½ tablespoons unsalted butter, softened

24 slices cocktail rye bread or 6 slices sandwich rye bread, crusts discarded and bread cut into 1½-inch squares

½ lb thinly sliced smoked salmon, cut into 24 pieces

¼ cup sour cream

24 small dill sprigs

Bring vinegar, water, and sugar just to a boil in a saucepan, stirring until sugar is dissolved, then cool. Pour over cucumber in a bowl and let stand, covered and chilled, at least 2 hours.

Drain pickled cucumber well. Butter 1 side of each slice of bread, then arrange 1 piece salmon then 3 cucumber slices decoratively on each square. Top with a very small dollop of sour cream and a dill sprig.

COOKS' NOTES

• Cucumber can marinate up to 1 day.

• Bread may be cut and wrapped tightly in plastic wrap 3 hours ahead.

MAKES **24** HORS D'OEUVRES

Green olive and almond tapenade

3 cups brine-cured green olives, pitted

1 cup fresh flat-leaf parsley

½ cup slivered almonds, toasted

¼ cup fresh lemon juice

1⅓ cups olive oil

Accompaniments: carrot sticks and toasted pita wedges or toasted baguette slices

Blend olives, parsley, almonds, and lemon juice in a food processor until finely chopped. With motor running, add oil in a stream, blending to form a paste.

MAKES ABOUT **3** CUPS

THIS RECIPE COMES FROM AMY SUE KECK OF SAN DIEGO, CALIFORNIA.

Lemongrass-rum iced tea

9 cups water

1½ cups sugar

10 large lemongrass stalks (1¼ lb), tough outer leaves discarded and lower 6 inches thinly sliced

2¼ cups light rum

1 (2-liter) bottle seltzer

Garnish: lime wedges

Bring 6 cups water, sugar, and lemongrass to a boil in a large saucepan, stirring until sugar is dissolved. Remove from heat and let stand, covered, 20 minutes.

Pour through a fine sieve into a large metal bowl, then stir in remaining 3 cups water. Chill tea until cold, then stir in rum.

Serve tea over ice and top with seltzer.

COOKS' NOTE

• Tea (without rum) may be made 1 day ahead and chilled, covered.

SERVES 10 TO 12

Tropical fruit punch

4 cups guava juice

2 cups papaya juice

2 cups pineapple juice

2 tablespoons fresh lime juice (preferably Key lime)

1 (2-liter) bottle seltzer

Stir together juices in a pitcher and chill until cold. Serve punch over ice and top with seltzer.

COOKS' NOTE

• Punch may be made 1 day ahead and chilled, covered.

MAKES 10 DRINKS

Finger food—how much is enough?

MANY HOSTS, even those who can plan and execute a dinner party for twelve with aplomb, find themselves at a loss when it comes to estimating how many hors d'oeuvres to make. Keep in mind the variety of dishes you want to prepare and the richness of each one. If you intend to serve a pre-dinner menu, be sure to keep it light; on the other hand, if you'd like your menu to serve as a buffet supper, add a miniature sweet to your assortment. Below is a very general, and generous, guideline.

Number of guests	Types of hors d'oeuvres	How many per person
8 to 10	at least 4	3 or 4
14 to 16	5 or 6	2 or 3
20 to 30	7 or 8	1 or 2

SERVES 8

Tequila limeade

Grilled shrimp with avocado
and roasted tomatillo salsa

Roasted red snapper fillets
with pumpkin seed sauce

Green rice

Orange, jícama,
and cilantro salad

Coconut lime sorbet

Pellegrini Alexander Valley
Carignan, Old Vines, 1998

St. Francis Sonoma County
Chardonnay 1999

Mexican dinner

OUR MEXICAN MENU presents a
modern take on classic flavors. Instead
of margaritas, there's tequila limeade;
avocado-tomatillo salsa with grilled
shrimp replaces guacamole and chips;
and for the main course, we offer an
uncommonly elegant roasted red snapper.
You'll find chiles, cilantro, lime juice, and
pumpkin seeds throughout, all used in
fresh and vibrant ways. Each dish is easy
enough to qualify as casual, yet sufficient-
ly sophisticated for entertaining. This is
Mexican food at its most subtle and
refined, without a *chimichanga* in sight.

Grilled shrimp with avocado and roasted tomatillo salsa

1 lb fresh tomatillos, husked and rinsed

1 small onion, quartered

4 garlic cloves, unpeeled

¼ cup packed fresh cilantro

2 fresh jalapeño chiles, seeded, if desired, and coarsely chopped

2 teaspoons salt, or to taste

3 firm-ripe California avocados

40 medium shrimp (about 1¼ lb), deveined and shelled, leaving tails intact

2 tablespoons vegetable oil

Special equipment: 8 (12-inch) bamboo skewers, soaked in water 1 hour

Preheat broiler.

Broil tomatillos, onion, and garlic on rack of a broiler pan 1 to 2 inches from heat, turning once, until softened and slightly charred, about 10 minutes. Peel garlic and pureé with tomatillos, onion, cilantro, jalapeños, and salt in a food processor until almost smooth. Transfer salsa to a bowl.

Halve and pit avocados and scoop flesh into tomatillo mixture. Mash avocados into mixture with a fork, leaving texture coarse.

Prepare grill for cooking.

Thread 5 shrimp onto each skewer, then brush with oil and season with salt. Grill until just cooked through, about 1 minute on each side.

Serve shrimp with salsa.

SERVES 8

Tequila limeade

1½ cups sugar

6 cups water

1½ cups fresh lime juice (preferably Key lime)

1½ cups tequila

1 (2-liter) bottle seltzer

Garnish: lime wedges

Simmer sugar and 3 cups water in a 3-quart saucepan, stirring until sugar is dissolved. Remove pan from heat and stir in remaining 3 cups water and lime juice.

Chill limeade until cold, then stir in tequila. Serve over ice and top with seltzer.

COOKS' NOTES

• You'll need about 36 Key limes or 10 regular limes to yield 1½ cups juice.

• Limeade (without tequila) may be made 1 day ahead and chilled, covered.

SERVES 8

Green rice

¾ lb fresh poblano chiles (4), seeded, deveined, and chopped

1 medium white onion, chopped

3 garlic cloves, minced

12 fresh flat-leaf parsley sprigs

12 fresh cilantro sprigs

2¾ cups chicken broth

2 cups long-grain white rice

¼ cup vegetable oil

¾ teaspoon salt

Purée chiles, onion, garlic, parsley, cilantro, and ½ cup broth in a blender until smooth as possible.

Cook rice in oil in a 4-quart heavy saucepan over moderately high heat, stirring, until pale golden, about 2 minutes. Add purée and cook over moderate heat, stirring, until liquid is evaporated, 2 to 4 minutes. Add salt and remaining 2¼ cups broth, then simmer, uncovered, until steam holes appear in rice, 10 to 12 minutes.

Cover pan and cook over very low heat until rice is tender and liquid is absorbed, about 15 minutes. Remove from heat and let stand, covered, 10 minutes, then fluff with a fork.

COOKS' NOTE

• Rice may be made 1 day ahead, cooled completely, then chilled, covered. To reheat, sprinkle with 2 tablespoons water in a shallow baking pan and cover with foil, then bake in a 350°F oven until hot, 12 to 15 minutes.

SERVES 8

Roasted red snapper fillets with pumpkin seed sauce

1 cup unsalted hulled (green) pumpkin seeds

2 cups chicken broth

2 *serrano* or jalapeño chiles, chopped, including seeds (3 tablespoons)

¼ cup fresh cilantro sprigs

½ cup finely chopped white onion

1 garlic clove, finely chopped

2 tablespoons vegetable oil

1 cup sour cream or crème fraîche

2 tablespoons heavy cream

8 (6-oz) red snapper fillets with skin

1 tablespoon olive oil

Preheat oven to 375°F.

Toast pumpkin seeds in a dry large heavy skillet over moderate heat, stirring, until puffed and beginning to pop, 3 to 4 minutes (do not let brown). Purée seeds, broth, chiles, cilantro, onion, and garlic in a blender until smooth.

Heat vegetable oil in a 2-quart heavy saucepan over moderately low heat until hot but not smoking, then add pumpkin seed sauce. Cook, stirring frequently, 10 minutes. Whisk together sour cream and heavy cream, then stir into sauce with salt and pepper to taste. Heat, stirring, until just hot (do not boil).

Brush fillets with olive oil and season with salt and pepper, then arrange, skin sides down, in 1 layer in an oiled shallow baking pan. Roast in middle of oven until just cooked through, 12 to 14 minutes.

Serve sauce over fish.

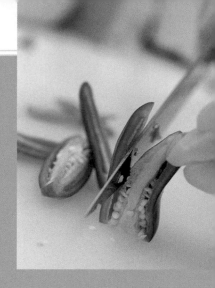

Clever cuts for peppers, etc.

WHO KNOWS WHERE we picked up this trick, but we thought it was high time to share it. Rather than cutting a chile or bell pepper in half, then carving out the seeds and ribs (they always seem to scatter all over the kitchen), simply lop off the sides. If you're prepping chiles, you've just minimized contact with the hot capsaicin. And if you want flat pieces of bell pepper for grilling, the technique is a natural there, too. You can also "fillet" a tomato, mango, or pineapple the same way.

–JANE DANIELS LEAR

COOKS' NOTES

• If small red snapper fillets are not available, use 6-oz pieces of fillet. These may be thicker and require a slightly longer cooking time, 14 to 20 minutes.

• Pumpkin seed sauce can be made 2 days ahead and chilled, covered. Reheat over moderately low heat, stirring, and thin with water if necessary (do not boil).

SERVES 8

Orange, jícama, and cilantro salad

3 tablespoons white-wine vinegar

½ teaspoon ground cumin

½ teaspoon sugar

¼ cup olive oil

6 navel oranges

2 medium jícama (1½ lb total)

⅔ cup cilantro

Whisk together vinegar, cumin, sugar, and salt and pepper to taste until sugar is dissolved, then whisk in oil.

Cut peel and pith from oranges. Halve oranges lengthwise, then cut crosswise into ¼-inch-thick slices. Transfer oranges and any accumulated juices to a large bowl. Peel and cut jícama into ¼-inch-thick sticks, about 3 inches long. Add to oranges with cilantro, then toss with dressing.

COOKS' NOTE

• Oranges and jícama may be cut 4 hours ahead and kept separately, covered tightly with plastic wrap and chilled.

SERVES 8

Coconut lime sorbet

1¼ cups water

1 cup sugar

1½ cups canned unsweetened coconut milk (from a 14-oz can)

1 cup fresh lime juice

1 cup sweetened flaked coconut, toasted

Special equipment: an ice-cream maker

Boil water and sugar in a saucepan, stirring, until sugar is dissolved. Remove pan from heat and stir in coconut milk, then cool.

Stir together coconut milk mixture and lime juice and freeze in ice-cream maker. Transfer sorbet to a bowl and stir in ½ cup flaked coconut. Transfer to an airtight container and put in freezer to harden.

Serve sorbet sprinkled with remaining ½ cup flaked coconut.

COOKS' NOTE

• We prefer Thai Kitchen brand coconut milk for this recipe.

SERVES 8

Simple summer buffet

SATURDAY NIGHT and the gang's
coming over to watch the fireworks, or the
ball game, or perhaps for no particular
reason at all. Whatever the situation, the
time is right for a casual buffet. Set up
shop in the kitchen and let everyone help
themselves to summery dishes that, for
the most part, can be served at room temperature. Everything tastes fresh and light.
Cheers to the hassle-free host.

Asparagus, cucumbers, and sugar snap peas with herb garlic dip

2½ cups plain yogurt

1 cup fresh flat-leaf parsley

1 tablespoon chopped fresh tarragon

½ teaspoon minced garlic

2 tablespoons fresh lemon juice

1 lb thin asparagus, trimmed

½ lb sugar snap peas, trimmed

1 tablespoon extra-virgin olive oil

3 Kirby cucumbers, cut lengthwise into spears

MAKE DIP:

Drain yogurt in a cheesecloth-lined sieve or colander set over a bowl, covered and chilled, at least 8 hours. Pulse yogurt in a food processor with parsley, tarragon, garlic, juice, and salt and pepper to taste until herbs are finely chopped and yogurt is pale green.

BLANCH VEGETABLES:

Blanch asparagus in a large saucepan of boiling salted water 1 minute. Immediately transfer with tongs to a bowl of ice water to stop cooking. Drain well in a colander and pat dry. Return water in saucepan to a boil and blanch peas 30 seconds. Drain in sieve and immediately plunge into ice water to stop cooking. Drain well and pat dry.

Drizzle oil over dip and serve with vegetables.

COOKS' NOTES

• Yogurt can drain up to 1 day.

• Dip may be made 1 day ahead and chilled, covered.

• Asparagus and peas may be blanched 1 day ahead and chilled in sealable plastic bags.

SERVES **8**

Broccoli rabe, black olive, and smoked mozzarella pizza

1 frozen puff pastry sheet (from a 17¼-oz package), thawed

½ lb broccoli rabe, 1 inch trimmed from stems

⅓ cup drained Kalamata or other brine-cured black olives, pitted and chopped

2 garlic cloves, minced

1 tablespoon fresh lemon juice

6 oz smoked mozzarella, coarsely grated

1 tablespoon extra-virgin olive oil

Roll out pastry sheet on a lightly floured surface with a floured rolling pin into a 14- by 12-inch rectangle. Transfer to a parchment-lined baking sheet and prick all over with a fork. Chill pastry, covered, at least 30 minutes.

Preheat oven to 400°F.

Blanch broccoli rabe in a saucepan of boiling salted water 30 seconds. Immediately transfer with tongs to a bowl of ice water to stop cooking. Drain well in a colander and pat dry. Cut broccoli rabe into ½-inch pieces and transfer to a bowl. Add olives, garlic, lemon juice, and salt and pepper to taste and toss well.

Bake pastry in middle of oven until golden, 15 to 20 minutes. Sprinkle mozzarella evenly over pastry, leaving a ½-inch border on all sides. Spread broccoli rabe evenly on top of cheese and bake in middle of oven 10 minutes, or until heated through. Drizzle oil over pizza.

COOKS' NOTE

• Puff pastry may be rolled out and chilled up to 1 day.

SERVES **8**

Fattoosh

Lebanese bread-and-tomato salad

3 (6-inch) pita loaves with pockets

2 tablespoons fresh lemon juice

1½ teaspoons pomegranate molasses (optional)

½ cup extra-virgin olive oil

1½ cups fresh flat-leaf parsley, torn if large

¾ cup fresh mint, torn if large

⅓ cup fresh purslane leaves (optional)

3 lb tomatoes, cut into wedges

Preheat oven to 375°F.

Split pita loaves and toast on a baking sheet in middle of oven until golden, 10 to 15 minutes. Cool on a rack, then break into bite-size pieces.

Whisk together lemon juice, pomegranate molasses, and salt to taste in a serving bowl, then whisk in oil until emulsified.

Add pita to dressing with remaining ingredients and toss to combine. Let stand 15 minutes. Toss again and serve.

COOKS' NOTE

• Salad is best served within 30 minutes (otherwise the bread will absorb too much of the tomato juices).

SERVES 8

Grilled flank steak

3 lb flank steaks

⅓ cup white-wine vinegar

¾ cup olive oil

1½ tablespoons minced fresh rosemary

3 garlic cloves, minced

2 teaspoons salt

1 teaspoon black pepper

Lightly pierce steaks all over with a sharp fork or knife. Whisk together remaining ingredients and transfer to a large resealable heavy-duty plastic bag. Add steaks and seal, pressing out excess air. Marinate steaks at least 6 hours or up to 1 day.

Prepare grill for cooking.

Grill steaks on an oiled rack set 5 to 6 inches over glowing coals, turning once, about 12 minutes for medium-rare. Transfer to a cutting board and let stand 5 minutes. Thinly slice steaks diagonally across the grain.

COOKS' NOTES

• Since flank steak is thicker on one end, the thin end will be cooked medium.

• Steaks may also be grilled in a well-seasoned ridged grill pan. Cut them into pieces to fit the pan and cook about 10 minutes, turning once.

SERVES 8

Orzo, pine nut, and feta salad

1 lb orzo

3 tablespoons fresh lemon juice

½ cup olive oil

½ cup pine nuts, toasted

1¼ cups feta (6 oz), crumbled

1 cup thinly sliced scallion greens

Cook orzo in a 6- to 8-quart pot of boiling salted water until tender, then drain well in a colander.

Whisk together lemon juice, oil, and salt and pepper to taste in a large bowl, then add hot orzo and toss. Cool orzo, then toss with pine nuts, feta, and scallion greens. Season with salt and pepper.

COOKS' NOTE

• Orzo may be tossed with dressing 1 hour ahead and kept at room temperature, covered. Toss with remaining ingredients just before serving.

SERVES 8

Pistachio brown-sugar cookies

1½ cups all-purpose flour

¾ teaspoon baking powder

¼ teaspoon salt

2 sticks (1 cup) unsalted butter, softened

1 cup packed light brown sugar

1 large egg yolk

1 teaspoon vanilla

1 cup salted natural pistachios, toasted and chopped

Preheat oven to 350°F.

Sift together flour, baking powder, and salt. Beat together butter and sugar with an electric mixer until pale and fluffy, then beat in yolk and vanilla. Mix in flour mixture at low speed until just blended, then stir in nuts.

Drop tablespoons of batter 3 inches apart onto ungreased baking sheets and bake in batches in middle of oven until just golden, 10 to 12 minutes. Cool cookies on baking sheets 5 minutes, then transfer carefully to racks to cool.

COOKS' NOTE

• Cookies keep 1 week in an airtight container.

MAKES ABOUT **30** COOKIES

Grape gelées with berries

2 envelopes unflavored gelatin

5 cups white grape juice

½ cup sugar

2 cups raspberries

2 cups blueberries

Sprinkle gelatin over 1 cup grape juice and sugar in a small saucepan and soften 1 minute. Heat over moderately high heat, stirring until gelatin and sugar are dissolved. Stir together with remaining 4 cups grape juice in a bowl, then chill until thickened to consistency of raw egg white, 40 to 45 minutes.

Stir in berries and spoon mixture into 8 (1-cup) stemmed glasses. Chill until set, about 3 hours.

COOKS' NOTE

• Gelées may be made 2 days ahead and chilled, covered.

SERVES **8**

Pistachios

IF YOU'RE A PISTACHIO LOVER, do yourself a favor and seek out the ones from Iran—they are slowly trickling into stores after being banned for more than 20 years. The flavor is beyond intense; it's undiluted somehow (we're talking ur-pistachio). It's also more rounded and a little sweeter than that of Turkish pistachios. Both Iranian and Turkish nuts are very dry and very crisp. California pistachios are quite sweet in comparison and lack depth of flavor. They're also a slightly tougher chew. Iranian pistachios are available by mail order from Kalustyan's (212-685-3451).

—JANE DANIELS LEAR

From top to bottom:
Turkish, Iranian, Californian

SERVES 6

Belgian endive spears with
fontina and walnut filling

White bean, olive, and
rosemary purée on toasts

Parsnip parmesan ravioli with
mushroom ragout

Radicchio and boston lettuce
with garlic vinaigrette

Balsamic-roasted pears with
pepper and honey

Ponzi Willamette Valley
Pinot Noir 1998

Fall vegetarian dinner

AS SOON AS THE AUTUMN wind turns even slightly chilly, vegetarians and meat-eaters alike begin to crave more robust dinners, the kinds of meals that truly satiate. Here's a menu that offers the best of the season's bounty, like parsnips and pears, while also taking advantage of a few pantry staples, namely canned white beans and tomatoes. This is an altogether different breed of comfort food—by turns healthy and modern, yet soul-satisfying to the very core.

Belgian endive spears with fontina and walnut filling

¼ lb Fontina, cut into ¼-inch cubes

¾ cup walnuts, toasted and finely chopped

⅓ cup fresh flat-leaf parsley, finely chopped

1 teaspoon fresh lemon juice, or to taste

1 tablespoon olive oil

18 Belgian endive leaves (from 3 endives)

Toss together cheese, walnuts, parsley, lemon juice, oil, and salt and pepper to taste. Spoon some of mixture onto base of each endive leaf.

COOKS' NOTE

• Endive may be separated into leaves 4 hours ahead and chilled in resealable plastic bags.

SERVES 6

White bean, olive, and rosemary purée on toasts

12 (½-inch-thick) slices Italian or French bread

5 tablespoons extra-virgin olive oil

⅓ cup finely chopped red onion

2 cups canned *cannellini* or other white beans, rinsed and drained well

1 tablespoon fresh lemon juice

½ cup finely chopped Kalamata or other brine-cured black olives

1½ teaspoons minced fresh rosemary

1 teaspoon finely grated fresh lemon zest

1 garlic clove, minced

Preheat oven to 375°F.

Put bread slices on a baking sheet, then brush tops with 2 tablespoons oil and season lightly with salt. Toast bread in middle of oven until crisp but still soft inside, about 12 minutes, then transfer to a rack to cool.

Soak onion in water to cover 15 minutes. Drain well and pat dry with paper towels.

Coarsely purée beans with remaining 3 tablespoons oil and lemon juice in a food processor, then stir together with onion, olives, rosemary, zest, garlic, and salt and pepper to taste.

Serve purée with toasts.

COOKS' NOTE

• Purée may be made 4 hours ahead and chilled, covered. Bring to room temperature before serving.

SERVES 6

Parsnip parmesan ravioli with mushroom ragout

2 tablespoons unsalted butter

2 tablespoons olive oil

1 medium onion, thinly sliced

1 lb portobello mushrooms, caps (halved if large) and stems thinly sliced

¾ lb white mushrooms, thinly sliced

2 garlic cloves, minced

2½ teaspoons chopped fresh sage

1 (28- to 32-oz) can whole tomatoes, drained, reserving juice, and coarsely chopped

2 lb parsnips, peeled and cut into 1-inch pieces

½ cup freshly grated parmesan (2 oz)

30 won ton wrappers, thawed if frozen

MAKE MUSHROOM RAGOUT:

Heat butter and oil in a large heavy pot over moderate heat until butter is melted, then cook onion, stirring, until softened, about 5 minutes. Stir in all mushrooms, garlic, 1 teaspoon sage, and salt and pepper to taste and cook, stirring, until liquid mushrooms give off is evaporated, about 15 minutes. Stir in tomatoes with reserved juice and cook, uncovered, stirring occasionally, until sauce is thickened, about 30 minutes.

MAKE RAVIOLI FILLING:

Cook parsnips in a saucepan of boiling salted water to cover by 2 inches, uncovered, until very tender, about 15 minutes, then drain well. Purée parsnips in a food processor with parmesan, remaining 1½ teaspoons sage, and salt and pepper to taste until smooth, then cool.

ASSEMBLE RAVIOLI:

Put 1 wrapper on a lightly floured surface and mound 1 level tablespoon filling in center. Brush edges of wrapper with water and fold wrapper diagonally in half to form a triangle, pressing around filling to force out air. Transfer ravioli to a dry kitchen towel to drain, and make more in same manner, transferring to towel and turning occasionally to dry slightly.

COOK RAVIOLI:

Heat ragout in a saucepan over low heat, stirring occasionally, until hot. Cook ravioli in 3 batches in gently boiling salted water until they rise to surface and are tender, about 6 to 8 minutes. (Do not let water boil vigorously once ravioli have been added.) Transfer ravioli as cooked with a spoon to shallow baking pans, arranging in 1 layer, with about ½ inch cooking water. Keep warm, covered.

Transfer ravioli with a slotted spoon to 6 serving plates and top with ragout.

COOKS' NOTES

• Ragout may be made 2 days ahead, cooled completely, and chilled, covered.

• Filling may be made 1 day ahead and chilled, covered.

MAKES **30** RAVIOLI (SERVING **6** GENEROUSLY)

Radicchio and boston lettuce with garlic vinaigrette

2 large garlic cloves, minced and mashed to a paste with 1 teaspoon salt

2½ tablespoons white-wine vinegar

⅓ cup olive oil

3 heads Boston lettuce, torn into bite-size pieces (8 cups)

2 heads radicchio, torn into bite-size pieces (4 cups)

Whisk together garlic paste, vinegar, and pepper to taste, then whisk in oil until emulsified.

Toss lettuce and radicchio with garlic vinaigrette.

COOKS' NOTES

• Vinaigrette may be made 1 day ahead and chilled, covered.

• Whole lettuce and radicchio leaves may be rinsed and spun dry 1 day ahead, then chilled, wrapped in paper towels, and kept in resealable plastic bags.

SERVES 6

Balsamic-roasted pears with pepper and honey

3 tablespoons unsalted butter

3 firm-ripe Bosc pears, halved lengthwise and cored

4½ tablespoons balsamic vinegar

6 oz Manchego or mild fresh goat cheese, cut into 6 pieces and at room temperature

¼ cup plus 2 tablespoons honey

Preheat oven to 400°F.

Melt butter in an 8-inch square glass baking dish in middle of oven, about 3 minutes. Arrange pears, cut sides down, in 1 layer in butter and roast in middle of oven until tender, about 20 minutes. Pour vinegar over pears and roast 5 minutes more.

Transfer pears, cut sides down, to serving plates with cheese and spoon some of juices from baking dish over pears. Drizzle pears and cheese with honey and sprinkle with pepper.

SERVES 6

THIS SWEET-YET-SAVORY DESSERT WAS INSPIRED BY CHEF ALAIN RONDELLI'S COMBINATION OF PEARS, ROQUEFORT, AND PEPPER.

Dinner by the fire

ALL THE ELEMENTS are in place—
a definite chill in the air, fallen leaves,
maybe even some snow. Dinner should be
substantial; the setting, warm and cozy.
To keep things simple, try making the
carbonnade à la Flamande the day before.
Then you can assemble layers of ultra-
thin potato slices for the crisp and buttery
pommes Anna just before your guests
arrive. Since you don't have the opportu-
nity to relax by the fire every night, you'll
want to savor every minute.

Hot cider with rum

36 to 48 oz apple cider or juice

6 oz dark rum (¾ cup)

Garnish: thinly sliced apples

Heat cider until hot and pour into 6 mugs. Stir 2 tablespoons rum into each mug.

COOKS' NOTE

• For a cold version, pour 2 tablespoons rum over ice in a large glass and top off with 6 to 8 ounces apple juice or sparkling cider.

SERVES 6

Honey-roasted peppered pecans

¼ cup honey

2 teaspoons black pepper

1 teaspoon salt

¼ teaspoon ground allspice

½ lb pecan halves (2 cups)

2 tablespoons sugar

Preheat oven to 350°F.

Stir together honey, pepper, salt, and allspice, then add pecans, tossing to coat well. Spread pecans in 1 layer in a shallow (1-inch-deep) baking pan and sprinkle with sugar. Bake in middle of oven 15 minutes, then stir pecans and bake 5 minutes more. Transfer to a sheet of wax or parchment paper to cool and, working quickly, separate pecans with a fork while still warm. Serve at room temperature.

SERVES 6

Brussels sprouts with caraway seeds

3 (10-oz) cartons Brussels sprouts, trimmed and halved lengthwise

2 tablespoons olive oil

1 tablespoon unsalted butter

1 teaspoon caraway seeds

Cook Brussels sprouts in a 4- to 6-quart pot of boiling salted water until tender, 8 to 10 minutes, then drain in a colander.

While sprouts cook, heat oil and butter in a small heavy saucepan over moderately low heat until butter is melted. Cook caraway seeds, stirring, until a shade darker, 2 to 3 minutes.

Toss Brussels sprouts with caraway butter and salt and pepper to taste.

SERVES 6

Carbonnade à la flamande

Beef and onions braised in beer

- 2 (12-oz) bottles Pilsner beer
- 2 cups beef broth
- 1½ tablespoons light brown sugar
- 3½ lb boneless chuck fillet roast, cut into 1½-inch pieces
- 5 tablespoons vegetable oil
- 7 medium onions (3 lb), thinly sliced
- 2 garlic cloves, finely chopped
- 4 fresh flat-leaf parsley sprigs
- 2 thyme sprigs
- 1 bay leaf (not California)
- 1½ tablespoons unsalted butter
- 1½ tablespoons all-purpose flour

Heat beer, broth, and sugar in a 6- to 8-quart heavy ovenproof pot over high heat, stirring until sugar is dissolved, then remove from heat.

Pat beef dry and season with salt and pepper. Heat 2 tablespoons oil in a heavy 10- to 12-inch skillet over moderately high heat until hot but not smoking, then brown beef in batches, without crowding, adding another tablespoon oil if necessary. Transfer to pot with beer broth.

Preheat oven to 325°F.

Cook half of onions in 1 tablespoon oil in skillet over moderately high heat, stirring occasionally, until golden brown, 7 to 10 minutes, then transfer to pot. Cook remaining onions in remaining tablespoon oil in same manner. Add garlic and cook, stirring, 1 minute, then transfer to pot.

Stir in parsley, thyme, and bay leaf and bring beef to a simmer. Braise, covered, in middle of oven until very tender, 2½ to 3 hours.

Transfer beef and onions to a bowl with a slotted spoon and discard parsley, thyme, and bay leaf. Stir butter and flour together to form a paste, then whisk into sauce. Simmer sauce, whisking constantly, until thickened slightly, about 3 minutes, and season with salt and pepper. Stir beef and onions into sauce.

COOKS' NOTE

- Braised beef may be made 1 day ahead, cooled completely, uncovered, then chilled, covered.

SERVES 6

Pommes anna

Crusty potato cake

- 3 lb russet (baking) potatoes
- 2 sticks (1 cup) unsalted butter, clarified (procedure follows)
- 1½ teaspoons salt
- 1 teaspoon black pepper

Preheat oven to 400°F.

Peel potatoes and cut crosswise into 1⁄16-inch-thick slices using a mandoline or other manual slicer, transferring slices to a large bowl of cold water. Drain and pat dry. Toss potatoes with ¾ cup butter, salt, and pepper in large bowl until coated well, then arrange 1 layer of potato slices in each of 2 greased shallow baking pans (about one fourth of potatoes). Bake in upper and lower third of oven until just tender and flexible but not golden, about 5 minutes. Bake remaining potatoes in same manner.

While second batch of potatoes bakes, brush bottom of a well-seasoned 10-inch cast-iron or nonstick skillet with some remaining butter and put 1 baked potato slice in center. Arrange 1 layer of slices around center slice in a concentric circle, overlapping slightly. Arrange another layer in same manner but reversing direction of circle so layers are even. Continue layering with remaining baked slices, reversing direction with each new layer. Repeat layering process with each batch of potatoes as baked.

Cover surface of potatoes with a round of buttered foil and press down firmly. If using a nonstick skillet with a plastic handle, wrap the handle in a double thickness of foil. Weight potatoes with a heavy lid (about 1 pound) or a cake pan (filled with 1 pound dried beans) that just fits inside skillet, then bake in middle of oven 30 minutes. Remove lid and foil and bake potatoes until tender and edge of potato cake is golden, 10 to 20 minutes more.

Run a thin knife around edge of skillet. Invert potato cake onto a plate and cut into wedges.

SERVES 6

To clarify butter

Unsalted butter, cut into 1-inch pieces

Melt butter in a heavy saucepan over low heat. Remove from heat and let stand 3 minutes. Skim froth and strain butter through a sieve lined with a double thickness of rinsed and squeezed cheesecloth into a bowl, leaving milky solids in bottom of pan. Pour clarified butter into a jar or crock and store, covered, in refrigerator.

COOKS' NOTES

- Butter keeps, covered and chilled, indefinitely.

- When clarified, butter loses about one fourth of its original volume.

Lemon molasses chess pie

Pastry dough (recipe follows)

2 lemons

4 large eggs

1¼ cups sugar

½ stick (¼ cup) unsalted butter, melted and cooled

¼ cup unsulfured molasses

¼ cup heavy cream

2 tablespoons yellow cornmeal

⅛ teaspoon salt

Accompaniment: lightly sweetened whipped cream

Special equipment: pie weights or raw rice for weighting shell

Roll out dough into a 12-inch round (about ⅛ inch thick) on a lightly floured surface with a floured rolling pin. Fit dough into a 9-inch (1-quart) glass pie plate and trim edge. Crimp edge decoratively and prick bottom of shell in several places with a fork. Chill shell until firm, about 30 minutes.

Preheat oven to 375°F.

Line shell with foil and fill with pie weights or raw rice. Bake in middle of oven 25 minutes. Transfer to a rack and carefully remove weights or rice and foil, then cool shell.

Increase temperature to 450°F.

Finely grate enough lemon zest to measure 1 tablespoon and squeeze enough juice to measure 3 tablespoons. Beat together eggs and sugar in a bowl with an electric mixer until thick and pale, then beat in butter, zest, juice, and remaining ingredients at medium speed until combined. (Custard will be thin.) Pour into shell.

Put pie in middle of oven. Reduce temperature to 325°F. Bake until just set in center, 35 to 40 minutes, and cool completely on rack. Serve pie at room temperature.

COOKS' NOTE

• Pie may be made 6 hours ahead and kept, uncovered, at cool room temperature.

Pastry dough

1¼ cups all-purpose flour

¾ stick (6 tablespoons) cold unsalted butter

2 tablespoons cold vegetable shortening

¼ teaspoon salt

2 to 4 tablespoons ice water

Blend together flour, butter, shortening, and salt in a bowl with your fingertips or a pastry blender (or pulse in a food processor) until most of mixture resembles coarse meal with rest in small (roughly pea-size) lumps. Drizzle evenly with 2 tablespoons ice water and gently stir with a fork (or pulse in a processor) until incorporated. Gently squeeze a small handful: It should hold together without crumbling apart. If it doesn't, add more water, 1 tablespoon at a time, stirring (or pulsing) after each addition until incorporated, and continue to test. (Do not overwork dough or it will become tough.)

Turn dough out onto a work surface. With heel of your hand, smear once in a forward motion to help distribute fat. Gather dough and form it, rotating on a work surface, into a disk. Wrap disk in wax paper and chill until firm, at least 1 hour.

COOKS' NOTE

• Dough can be chilled up to 1 day.

MAKES ENOUGH DOUGH FOR A 9-INCH PIE

ADDING A CHEESE COURSE to a simple casual menu can be a lovely way to complement the food, especially when you have plenty of time to linger over another bottle of wine. But which cheeses to offer? You may want to highlight the products of a particular country (for example, a selection of French cheeses would be heavenly after the *carbonnade à la Flamande* and *pommes Anna* in our Dinner by the Fire). Or, if particular types of cheeses, like Cheddars or blues, are your passion, perhaps you'll want to serve an assortment of those. Or, to satisfy an array of palates, an eclectic assortment of textures and flavors might be best. Be sure to include a variety of crackers, a crusty baguette, or a walnut-studded whole-wheat. Grapes, fresh figs, or pears (cut in halves or quarters with a stainless-steel knife to prevent discoloration) can be added (in lieu of dessert). Here are a few of our cheese favorites—keep in mind that there remains some controversy in the U. S. surrounding consumption of cheeses made from raw (unpasteurized) milk:

Goat Cheeses

Chabichou du Poitou (Poitou, France)—Look for Le Chevrot, a brand available in the U.S. Comes both raw (unpasteurized) and pasteurized, with a stark-white, creamy interior and a sharp citrusy flavor. Beige or light brown rind with faint mold.

Pouligny Saint-Pierre (Berry, France)—A raw cheese similar in shape to Valencay but taller. When aged, it has a slightly crumbly yet moist and creamy interior, a salty-sour tang, and blue mold on the rind. Classic *chèvre*.

Valencay (Berry, France)—Available both raw and pasteurized. Short, four-sided, truncated pyramid sometimes covered in (edible) ash. The white interior is smooth, soft, and mild; flavor intensifies and rind hardens as the cheese ages.

Soft Cheeses

Pierre Robert (Brie, France)—A triple-crème pasteurized cow's-milk cheese with a luscious, mild flavor. As it ripens, the rind becomes a mottled beige-brown.

Taleggio (Lombardy, Italy)—A cow's-milk cheese that is available both raw and pasteurized. Refined, mild salty flavor; musky rind.

Firm/Hard Cheeses

Farmhouse Cheddar (southern England)—A firm cow's-milk cheese that comes both raw and pasteurized. Two superb examples are Keen's (sharp flavor, closer to what most Americans are used to) and Montgomery (a little fruitier).

Parmigiano-Reggiano (Emilia-Romagna, Italy)—A raw cow's-milk cheese with a granular texture. Flavor is fruitiest when cheese is no more than two years old.

Blue Cheeses

Cabrales (Asturias, Spain)—Mixture of cow's, goat's, and sheep's milk; comes both raw and pasteurized. Rich flavor and a crumbly texture similar to that of Roquefort. Striking blue-purple veining.

Gorgonzola Dolce (Lombardy, Italy)—A mild, almost sweet raw cow's-milk cheese with a creamy texture; differs from aged Gorgonzola (Gorgonzola *naturale*), which is sharper and firmer.

Last minute dinner

FAVORITE RECIPES are like old friends—they can be counted on at a moment's notice, and the best of them never let you down. For this menu, we've collected a half dozen of our most tried-and-true, absolutely reliable recipes. After a bit of rummaging in your pantry and one quick trip to the grocery store, you'll have everything you need (except, of course, your dearest friends, but they should be equally easy to rustle up.)

Herbed goat cheese and sun-dried tomato spread

½ lb mild soft goat cheese, softened

3 tablespoons finely chopped drained sun-dried tomatoes in oil

1½ teaspoons minced fresh thyme

1 teaspoon minced fresh rosemary

1 small shallot, minced

¼ cup extra-virgin olive oil

Accompaniment: toasts or crackers

Beat cheese with an electric mixer until smooth, then stir in remaining ingredients and salt and pepper to taste.

COOKS' NOTE

• Spread may be made 2 days ahead and chilled, covered. Bring to room temperature before serving.

SERVES 4

Superquick hors d'oeuvre

PERHAPS THE MOST IRRESISTIBLE, and nutritious, cocktail nibble going these days is *edamame*—young, tender soybeans that are usually eaten straight from the pod. (Gently suck the beans into your mouth, and when serving them, don't forget to provide a bowl for the pods.) All they require is a quick steam or boil followed by a plunge into ice water, a quick drain, then a liberal dose of sea salt (or a gourmet salt of your choice). They are a great last-minute hors d'oeuvre.

Look for frozen *edamame* at your grocery store.

—JANE DANIELS LEAR

Rib-eye steaks with curried salt

1 tablespoon kosher salt

3½ teaspoons curry powder

4 (¾-inch-thick) beef rib-eye steaks

¼ cup water

Preheat oven to 300°F.

Stir together salt and curry powder. Pat 2 steaks dry and sprinkle both sides evenly with half of curried salt.

Heat a well-seasoned 10-inch cast-iron skillet over moderately high heat until hot but not smoking, then sear steaks 4 to 5 minutes on each side, or until an instant-read thermometer inserted horizontally into thickest part of meat registers 130°F for medium-rare. Transfer steaks to an ovenproof dish and keep warm in oven. Wipe out skillet. Prepare and cook remaining steaks in same manner.

Add water and any meat juices that have accumulated in dish to skillet and deglaze skillet by boiling over high heat, stirring and scraping up brown bits, until reduced to about 4 tablespoons. Spoon juices over meat.

SERVES 4

Photo on page 48

Broccoli rabe in garlic butter

2 lb broccoli rabe (2 bunches), hollow stems discarded

2 tablespoons unsalted butter

2 garlic cloves, chopped

Cook broccoli rabe in a large pot of boiling salted water until just tender, about 4 minutes, then drain in a colander.

Melt butter in same pot over moderate heat, then cook garlic, stirring, until fragrant, about 30 seconds. Add broccoli rabe, tossing gently to coat, and season with salt and pepper.

SERVES 4 GENEROUSLY

Roast parsnips

2 lb parsnips, peeled and cut diagonally into ¼-inch-thick slices

2 tablespoons vegetable oil

Preheat oven to 450°F.

Toss parsnips with vegetable oil and salt to taste in a shallow (1-inch-deep) baking pan and roast in middle of oven, turning over halfway through cooking, until golden and tender, 30 to 35 minutes total.

SERVES 4

Broiled apples with maple calvados sauce

4 Fuji or Royal Gala apples, peeled, cored, and each cut into 16 wedges

¼ cup fresh lemon juice

4 tablespoons sugar

2 tablespoons unsalted butter

⅓ cup pure maple syrup

2 tablespoons Calvados

Accompaniment: premium-quality vanilla ice cream

Preheat broiler.

Toss apples with lemon juice and 2 tablespoons sugar. Melt butter in a shallow baking pan 6 inches from heat. Remove from oven and tilt pan back and forth to coat bottom completely with butter. Arrange apples in 1 layer in pan, then broil 6 inches from heat until edges are pale golden and apples are just tender, 8 to 10 minutes. Sprinkle remaining 2 tablespoons sugar over apples and broil until sugar is melted, 1 to 2 minutes.

While apples broil, boil maple syrup and Calvados 2 minutes.

Serve apples and ice cream topped with sauce.

SERVES 4

Napa cabbage, asian pear, and carrot salad

2 tablespoons fresh lemon juice

2 tablespoons olive oil

1 small Asian pear (½ lb), peeled, cored, and cut into 2-inch julienne strips

4 cups thinly sliced Napa cabbage (from 1 head)

2 carrots, cut into 2-inch julienne strips

Whisk together lemon juice, oil, and salt and pepper to taste and toss with pear, cabbage, and carrots.

SERVES 4

WITH THE ALARM CLOCK

turned off, you can sleep to
your heart's content, at least
until the thud of the Sunday
paper delivery wakes you.
And, since there's no reason
to rush out the door, a lux-
uriously long breakfast is
another pleasing possibility.
Should you want to invite
friends over today—for
breakfast, brunch, lunch, supper, or perhaps just afternoon
coffee—you'll have plenty of
options for supereasy menus
that seem to cook themselves.

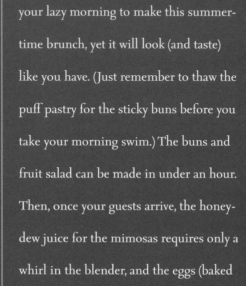

Beach house brunch

YOU WON'T HAVE TO SACRIFICE your lazy morning to make this summer-time brunch, yet it will look (and taste) like you have. (Just remember to thaw the puff pastry for the sticky buns before you take your morning swim.) The buns and fruit salad can be made in under an hour. Then, once your guests arrive, the honey-dew juice for the mimosas requires only a whirl in the blender, and the eggs (baked in lovely individual brioches) need only a few minutes of attention.

Honeydew mimosas

3 cups honeydew juice (recipe follows)

1 (750-ml) bottle chilled sparkling wine

Fill each of 6 Champagne flutes halfway with juice, then top with sparkling wine.

MAKES **6** DRINKS

Honeydew juice

1 (4-lb) honeydew melon, seeds and rind removed and flesh cut into 1-inch pieces

2 cups ice cubes

1 cup water

2 tablespoons sugar, or to taste

Blend half of melon with half of each remaining ingredient in a blender until very smooth. Pour juice into a pitcher and repeat with remaining ingredients.

COOKS' NOTE

• Though we use this melon juice to make our Mimosas, it is also delicious on its own. Simply add 1 teaspoon fresh lemon juice, or to taste, to each batch.

MAKES ABOUT **6** CUPS

Baked eggs in brioches

6 small brioches (each about 4 by 3 inches)

3 tablespoons unsalted butter, melted

6 large eggs

1 tablespoon chopped fresh tarragon
or chives

Preheat oven to 350°F.

Cut off tops of brioches (about 1 inch) and scoop out insides of bottoms to make a shell, leaving ¼ to ⅓ inch all around and being careful not to tear (cavity should be just big enough to fit a large egg). Brush insides and cut sides of tops with butter.

Arrange brioche shells in a muffin tin and season with salt and pepper. Crack an egg into each brioche and sprinkle with tarragon. Bake in lower third of oven 15 minutes. Arrange brioche tops, cut sides up, in a shallow baking pan and put in upper third of oven. Bake both bottoms and tops until eggs are cooked to desired degree of doneness and brioche tops are golden brown, 10 to 20 minutes.

Serve each brioche with its top for dipping in the egg.

COOKS' NOTE

• Serving the eggs with runny—not fully cooked—yolks may be of concern if there is a problem with salmonella in your area.

SERVES 6

Watermelon and mango with lime

1 (4-lb) piece watermelon (preferably seedless), rind and seeds discarded and fruit cut into 1-inch chunks

2 mangoes (1¾ lb), peeled, pitted, and cut into 1-inch chunks

1 tablespoon fresh lime juice, or to taste

1 teaspoon finely grated fresh lime zest

½ teaspoon sugar, or to taste

Toss together all ingredients and chill, covered, stirring occasionally, 20 minutes.

SERVES 6

Easy pecan sticky buns

¾ cup sugar

1 tablespoon plus 1 teaspoon cinnamon

1 cup pecans, toasted and chopped

2 frozen puff pastry sheets (from a 17¼-oz package), thawed

3 tablespoons plus 1 teaspoon milk

7 tablespoons confectioners sugar

Preheat oven to 375°F.

Stir together sugar, cinnamon, and pecans with a pinch of salt.

Roll 1 pastry sheet into an 18- by 12-inch rectangle (with a long side facing you) on a lightly floured surface with a floured rolling pin. Brush with 1 tablespoon milk, then sprinkle evenly with half of pecan sugar, leaving a ½-inch border on all sides. Starting with a long side, roll up rectangle to form an 18-inch log and trim ends. Cut log crosswise into 12 slices. Make another log in same manner and cut into slices.

Arrange slices, cut sides up, on 2 large greased baking sheets and bake in 2 batches in middle of oven until golden on top and centers are cooked through (buns will turn golden brown on bottom), about 20 minutes.

Stir together confectioners sugar and remaining milk until smooth and drizzle over warm buns.

SERVES 6

Cajun comforts

THE HEAVENLY AROMA of
simmering sausage, chicken, tomatoes,
corn, onions, bell peppers, and cayenne
will surely bring to mind the flavors of
Louisiana, home of Cajun cooking and
the original *maque choux*. Our variation on
this much-loved classic stew is a meal in
itself, especially when served with a loaf
of crusty bread. However, since southern
cooking is always about abundance, we
upped the ante with a few other favorites.
As host, all you need to add is a dash of
southern charm.

Chicken and sausage maque choux

6 ears corn

3 lb chicken thighs with skin, fat trimmed

1 tablespoon vegetable oil

¾ lb hot Italian sausage links, cut into small (½-inch-thick) slices

3 medium onions, chopped

1 orange or red bell pepper, chopped

1 green bell pepper, chopped

1 large celery rib, sliced

2 fresh thyme sprigs

½ teaspoon cayenne, or to taste

¾ lb cherry tomatoes (1½ pints), halved

¼ cup chopped fresh basil

Working over a large bowl, cut off corn kernels, then scrape each cob with a knife to extract juice. Discard cobs. Pat chicken dry and season with salt and pepper.

Heat oil in an 8-quart heavy pot over moderately high heat until hot but not smoking, then brown sausage, transferring to a plate. Brown chicken in batches, transferring to another plate.

Pour off all but 1 tablespoon fat from pot, then sauté onions, bell peppers, celery, thyme, cayenne, and salt to taste over moderately high heat, stirring occasionally, 4 minutes. Add corn with juices and cook, stirring, 2 minutes. Stir in tomatoes and sausage.

Nestle chicken into mixture and simmer, covered, stirring occasionally, until cooked through, about 40 minutes. (If the maque choux is too soupy, simmer uncovered until juices are reduced.) Stir in basil and salt and pepper to taste.

SERVES 6

Southern-style chopped slaw

¾ cup mayonnaise

1½ tablespoons cider vinegar

1 tablespoon sugar

2 teaspoons fresh lemon juice

½ teaspoon black pepper

1 (2-lb) head cabbage, cut into 2-inch pieces

¼ cup chopped fresh chives

¼ cup finely chopped fresh flat-leaf parsley

2 tablespoons finely chopped scallion greens

Whisk together mayonnaise, vinegar, sugar, lemon juice, and pepper in a large bowl.

Coarsely chop cabbage in batches in a food processor and transfer to bowl. Add chives, parsley, scallions, and salt to taste and stir until combined well.

COOKS' NOTE

• Slaw may be made 1 day ahead and chilled, covered.

SERVES 6

Brown-sugar pecan ice cream

1 cup packed light brown sugar

1 tablespoon cornstarch

⅛ teaspoon salt

3 large eggs

2 cups whole milk

2 teaspoons vanilla

2 cups chilled heavy cream

2 cups pecans (½ lb), toasted, cooled, and finely chopped

Special equipment: an ice-cream maker

Stir together brown sugar, cornstarch, and salt in a bowl, then whisk in eggs. Bring milk just to a boil in a 2½- to 3-quart heavy saucepan. Add hot milk to egg mixture in a slow stream, whisking, then pour into pan. Bring custard to a boil over moderate heat, whisking constantly, and boil, whisking, 1 minute. Stir in vanilla. (Custard will appear curdled.)

Chill custard until cold and stir in cream. Freeze custard, in batches if necessary, in ice-cream maker. Transfer to a large bowl and stir in pecans. Transfer ice cream to an airtight container and put in freezer to harden.

COOKS' NOTE

• Ice cream may be made 1 week ahead.

SERVES 6

Toasted-coconut cookies

1½ cups sweetened flaked coconut

1¼ cups all-purpose flour

1 teaspoon baking soda

½ teaspoon salt

1¼ sticks (½ cup plus 2 tablespoons) unsalted butter, softened

½ cup packed light brown sugar

¼ cup granulated sugar

1 large egg

1 teaspoon vanilla

Preheat oven to 375°F.

Spread coconut evenly in a shallow baking pan and lightly toast in middle of oven, stirring once, until pale golden, 4 to 5 minutes. Cool coconut.

Sift together flour, baking soda, and salt into a small bowl. Beat together butter and sugars in a large bowl with an electric mixer until light and fluffy. Beat in egg and vanilla, then stir in flour mixture and coconut until combined well.

Arrange teaspoons of dough about 1½ inches apart on ungreased baking sheets, then bake in batches in middle of oven until golden, 8 to 10 minutes. Cool cookies on sheets 1 minute and transfer with a metal spatula to racks to cool completely.

COOKS' NOTE

• Cookies keep in an airtight container at room temperature 1 week.

MAKES ABOUT 100 SMALL COOKIES

Ice-cream makers

HOMEMADE ICE CREAM is a treat, but, of course, you'll need to purchase an ice-cream maker for all custard-based recipes. Which one to buy? We did a bit of hands-on homework and here's what we found out. While price varies substantially, all the brands we tried make great ice cream. The lower-end machines (Krups and Cuisinart) are perfect for a kitchen with limited storage space. The Krups bowl and housing are integral, though, so you have to put the whole thing in the freezer. The Cuisinart, with its removable bowl, is more practical if your freezer is small. The high-end Simac is compact compared with the Mussos, and the (removable) bowl is easy to clean. The ultra-expensive Pola beats more air into the custard, resulting in a moussier texture and a higher yield, but it takes longer to churn. All the models lack a buzzer, to tell you that the churning has stopped. (The Mussos have timers, but they don't ring.) Now, that would be a bell or a whistle worth having.

–JANE DANIELS LEAR

Drop by for coffee

ONE OF THE NICEST things about Sundays is having time to catch-up with friends, so why not invite a few for coffee this afternoon? Just find the coziest, most comfortable spot to wile away the hours—the cushioned rockers on the porch, perhaps, or the old sofa in the den—and bring out a few extra-special treats. Little effort is required here. In fact, you probably have most of the ingredients on hand. You might want to serve everything all at once with the coffee, or, to stretch out the day, you might start with the scones and end with the sweeter chocolate-dipped biscotti. That way your guests can relish these goodies one by one.

Chocolate-dipped almond biscotti

1 cup all-purpose flour

½ cup sugar

1½ teaspoons finely grated fresh orange zest

½ teaspoon salt

¼ teaspoon baking soda

1 large whole egg

1 large egg white

½ teaspoon vanilla

¾ cup whole almonds with skins, toasted, cooled, and coarsely chopped

6 oz bittersweet chocolate (not unsweetened), melted

Preheat oven to 300°F.

Whisk together flour, sugar, zest, salt, and baking soda in a large bowl.

Beat together whole egg, egg white, and vanilla in another bowl with an electric mixer. Add flour mixture and beat until just combined (mixture will be moist). Stir in almonds.

Form dough into a 12- by 2-inch log with floured hands on a parchment-lined baking sheet, then bake in middle of oven until pale golden, about 45 minutes. Cool on baking sheet on a rack 10 minutes, then carefully peel parchment from log and transfer log to a cutting board. Cut log diagonally into ½-inch-thick slices in a sawing motion with a serrated knife. Arrange slices, cut sides down, on baking sheet and bake, turning slices once, until crisp, about 20 minutes total. Transfer to rack to cool.

Dip top (curved) edge of each biscotti in melted chocolate, letting excess drip off, then transfer, cut sides down, to a wax paper-lined baking sheet. Chill until chocolate is set, about 5 minutes.

COOKS' NOTE

• Biscotti may be made 1 day ahead and chilled, covered.

MAKES ABOUT **18** COOKIES

Currant tea scones

¼ cup boiling water

2 tea bags

1 cup dried currants

2 cups all-purpose flour

¼ cup plus 1 teaspoon sugar

3 teaspoons baking powder

½ teaspoon salt

1 stick (½ cup) cold unsalted butter, cut into ½-inch cubes

¾ cup half-and-half plus additional for brushing dough

Preheat oven to 400°F.

Pour boiling water into a small cup and steep tea bags 2 minutes. Remove tea bags, reserving them, and stir in currants. Sift together flour, ¼ cup sugar, baking powder, and salt into a bowl. Add butter and blend with your fingers until most of mixture resembles coarse meal with remainder in small (pea-size) lumps. Squeeze liquid from tea bags into cup and discard bags. Add ¾ cup half-and-half to flour mixture and stir with a fork until just combined and a sticky dough forms. Stir in currant mixture.

Form dough into 2 (5-inch) rounds on a lightly floured surface, then transfer to a buttered baking sheet. Brush dough lightly with additional half-and-half and sprinkle with remaining teaspoon sugar. Score dough ¼ inch deep into quarters with a knife.

Bake in middle of oven until golden, 20 to 25 minutes, then transfer to a rack to cool. Break scones along score marks and serve warm or at room temperature.

MAKES **8** SCONES

Nectarines and berries with anise

1¼ lb small nectarines, pitted and cut into ½-inch wedges

2½ cups blueberries (1¼ pints)

2 tablespoons superfine sugar

1 teaspoon Pernod

1 teaspoon fresh lemon juice

Stir together all ingredients and let stand, stirring occasionally, 20 minutes.

COOKS' NOTE

• Fruit can be prepared 1 hour ahead and chilled, covered.

SERVES **4**

Harvest dinner

IF EVER THERE WAS a great alfresco
menu filled with favorites that have
earned their place at the table, this is it.
Cold roast beef tenderloin, green goddess
dressing, creamy corn, and bacon—they're
all here in surprisingly wonderful combinations. The rustic free-form plum pie
looks especially like an old-time treasure.
It's even better topped with a scoop of
ginger ice cream for cold sweetness that at
the same time offers a touch of heat.
How's that for adding a modern stroke of
genius to a proven masterpiece?

Spinach, bacon, and goat cheese salad with pecans

½ lb sliced bacon

¾ cup pecans

3 tablespoons plus 2 teaspoons olive oil

2 tablespoons cider vinegar

1 (10-oz) bag baby spinach

2 oz goat cheese, crumbled

Cook bacon in a large skillet until crisp, then transfer with tongs to paper towels to drain. Reserve 3 tablespoons fat from skillet, discarding remainder. Crumble bacon.

Toast pecans in 2 teaspoons olive oil in skillet over moderate heat, stirring, until 1 shade darker, then transfer to paper towels to drain. Season nuts with salt and pepper and coarsely chop.

Heat reserved fat in a saucepan over moderately low heat until just warm. Remove pan from heat, then whisk in vinegar and remaining 3 tablespoons olive oil until emulsified. Season dressing with salt and pepper.

Toss bacon, spinach, cheese, and half of nuts with enough dressing to coat. Sprinkle salad with remaining nuts.

SERVES 6

Cold roast beef tenderloin with grilled vegetable salad

2 tablespoons kosher salt

1 tablespoon black pepper

1 (3-lb) beef tenderloin

2 large red onions, peeled and each cut into 8 wedges (do not trim root ends)

3 small yellow squash, halved lengthwise

2 red bell peppers, sides removed (see box on page 25)

3 tablespoons olive oil

2 tablespoons balsamic vinegar

½ cup chopped fresh cilantro

Preheat oven to 450°F.

Stir together kosher salt and pepper and sprinkle onto a large sheet of wax paper. Pat beef dry, then roll in seasoning until evenly coated. Put beef in a lightly oiled shallow roasting pan and roast in middle of oven until a meat thermometer inserted 2 inches into center of meat registers 130°F for medium-rare, about 35 minutes. Let meat stand in pan until cooled to room temperature. Wrap meat in plastic and chill overnight.

Prepare grill for cooking.

Toss together vegetables with oil and salt and pepper to taste until well coated. Grill in batches on a rack set 5 to 6 inches over glowing coals, turning once, until just tender, about 5 minutes. Transfer to a large plate to cool. Halve onion wedges, removing and discarding root ends. Cut squash crosswise into ½-inch-thick slices and cut peppers into 1-inch pieces. Toss vegetables with vinegar. Stir in cilantro just before serving.

Slice beef and serve with vegetables.

SERVES 6

Tomatoes with green goddess dressing

1 cup mayonnaise

½ cup chopped fresh flat-leaf parsley

¼ cup chopped fresh chives

2 tablespoons chopped scallion greens

1½ teaspoons anchovy paste

1 teaspoon white-wine vinegar

¼ teaspoon minced garlic

2 lb medium tomatoes, cut into wedges

Purée all ingredients except tomatoes in a food processor until pale green and smooth. Transfer to a bowl and thin with water, if desired.

Season tomatoes with salt and pepper and drizzle with dressing.

COOKS' NOTE

• Dressing may be made 1 day ahead and chilled, covered.

SERVES 6

Creamy corn with chives

6 ears corn

1½ teaspoons kosher salt

1 teaspoon cornstarch

Pinch of sugar (optional)

¼ cup plus 2 tablespoons finely chopped onion

3 tablespoons unsalted butter

½ cup water

3 tablespoons minced fresh chives

Working over a shallow bowl, cut off corn kernels, then scrape each cob with a knife to extract juice. Discard cobs. Purée 3 cups kernels, reserving remainder, and juice in a food processor 2 minutes. Force through a fine sieve into a bowl and discard solids. Stir in salt, cornstarch, and sugar.

Cook onion in butter in a saucepan over moderately low heat, stirring frequently, until softened. Add reserved kernels and water and simmer briskly, covered, stirring occasionally, until corn is crisp-tender, 4 to 5 minutes.

Stir corn purée, then stir into kernels. Bring to a boil, stirring, then simmer, stirring, until thickened, about 2 minutes. (If desired, thin with water.) Season with pepper and stir in chives.

SERVES 6

THIS IS CREAMY CORN WITH NO CREAM AT ALL. OUR TRICK? THE JUICE OF FRESHLY CUT CORN THICKENED WITH CORNSTARCH.

Rustic plum pie

1 stick (½ cup) plus 1 tablespoon cold
unsalted butter, cut into bits

1¼ cups all-purpose flour

⅔ cup plus 3 tablespoons sugar

½ teaspoon salt

2 to 5 tablespoons ice water

1¾ lb Italian prune plums, halved and pitted

1½ tablespoons cornstarch

2 tablespoons fresh lemon juice

1 tablespoon milk

Blend or pulse together butter, flour, 2 tablespoons sugar, and salt with a pastry blender or in
a food processor until mixture resembles coarse
meal. Add 2 tablespoons ice water and toss or
pulse until incorporated. Add enough remaining
ice water, 1 tablespoon at a time, tossing with a
fork or pulsing to incorporate, to form a dough.
Gather dough into a ball and smear with heel of
your hand in 3 or 4 forward motions on a work
surface. Form into a ball, then flatten into a disk.
Chill dough, wrapped in plastic wrap, 1 hour.

Preheat oven to 375°F.

Cut plums into ¾-inch-thick wedges and toss
with ⅔ cup sugar, cornstarch, and lemon juice in
a bowl.

Roll out dough into an 11-inch round (about ⅛
inch thick) on a lightly floured surface with a
floured rolling pin. Transfer to a 9-inch (1-quart)
glass pie plate. (Do not trim overhang.) Spoon
filling into shell and fold edge of dough over filling,
leaving center uncovered. Bake pie in middle of
oven 35 minutes. Brush crust with milk and
sprinkle with remaining tablespoon sugar. Bake
pie until filling is bubbling and crust is golden,
about 10 minutes more. Cool on a rack.

Ginger ice cream

¼ cup water

¾ cup sugar

¼ cup coarsely grated peeled fresh ginger

2 cups heavy cream

6 large egg yolks, lightly beaten

1 cup milk

1 teaspoon vanilla

½ cup chopped crystallized ginger (3 oz)

Special equipment: an ice-cream maker and
a candy thermometer

Simmer water, sugar, and fresh ginger in a 3-
quart heavy saucepan, stirring occasionally, until
sugar is dissolved, about 5 minutes. Add cream
and a pinch of salt and return to a simmer. Add
hot gingered cream to yolks in a stream, whisking constantly, then return to saucepan. Cook
custard over moderately low heat, stirring constantly, until thermometer registers 170°F and
custard coats the back of a spoon, about 2 minutes (do not let boil).

Pour custard through a fine sieve into cleaned
bowl, then stir in milk and vanilla. Cool custard,
stirring occasionally.

Freeze custard in an ice-cream maker, adding
crystallized ginger three fourths of way through
freezing process. Transfer to an airtight container
and freeze to harden.

COOKS' NOTE

• Ice cream keeps 1 week.

MAKES ABOUT 1½ QUARTS

Snowbound sunday

A MAJOR WINTER STORM arrives on cue and you're buried beneath the powdery white stuff. Why not leave the shoveling to the kids, then settle in for a nice long day in front of the fire with friends and some brandied toddies? Veal shanks with mashed potatoes will be ready by dinnertime after an ever so slow, aromatic braise, and a simple salad is the only accompaniment you'll need. Admittedly, our creamy cheesecake might be gilding the lily just a tad, but it's really heavenly. Besides, you can always go to the gym tomorrow.

Brandied cranberry toddies

3 cups cranberry juice cocktail

2 tablespoons light brown sugar

1 (1½-inch) piece fresh ginger, thinly sliced

1 (4-inch) cinnamon stick

¼ cup brandy or Cognac

Simmer juice, sugar, ginger, and cinnamon, covered, stirring occasionally, 15 minutes. Pour through a sieve into a heatproof pitcher, then stir in brandy.

SERVES **4**

Pesto cheese straws

1 frozen puff pastry sheet (from a 17¼-oz package), thawed

⅓ cup prepared pesto

¼ cup finely grated parmesan

Preheat oven to 450°F.

Roll pastry into a 17- by 12½-inch rectangle on a lightly floured surface with a floured rolling pin, then trim to measure 16 by 12 inches. Spread pesto evenly over pastry, then sprinkle with parmesan and season with pepper. Cut pastry crosswise into 1-inch-wide strips with a pizza wheel or sharp knife. Transfer strips 1 at a time (about 1 inch apart) to 2 large greased baking sheets, twisting each strip to enclose filling and pressing ends of each strip onto pan. Freeze strips 10 minutes.

Remove 1 pan of straws from freezer and bake in middle of oven until golden brown and crisp, 10 to 13 minutes. Loosen straws carefully with a spatula and transfer to racks to cool. Bake second pan of straws in same manner.

COOKS' NOTES

• If you don't have enough room in your freezer to freeze both sheets of pastry at the same time, put second sheet in freezer while first batch of breadsticks bakes.

• Cheese straws may be made 6 hours ahead, cooled completely, and kept at room temperature in an airtight container.

MAKES ABOUT 16 BREADSTICKS
Photo on back jacket

Romaine, parsley, and fennel salad with tapenade vinaigrette

2¼ teaspoons *tapenade* or other olive paste

1½ teaspoons balsamic vinegar

1½ teaspoons Dijon mustard

1 shallot, finely chopped

4½ tablespoons olive oil

1 small head romaine, cut crosswise into 1-inch-wide pieces

½ small head radicchio, coarsely chopped

¼ fennel bulb, core removed and bulb thinly sliced lengthwise

1 cup fresh flat-leaf parsley

Whisk together *tapenade*, vinegar, mustard, and shallot, then add oil in a slow stream, whisking until emulsified.

Toss remaining ingredients in a bowl with enough dressing to coat and season with salt and pepper.

SERVES 4

Braised veal shanks with mashed potatoes and tomato-onion jus

THERE'S NO
WINE OR
OTHER LIQUID
CALLED FOR
HERE. THE
VEAL COOKS
IN THE JUICES
EXUDED BY
THE TOMATOES
AND ONIONS.

4 (2-inch-thick) meaty crosscut veal shanks (osso buco; 1 lb each), tied with kitchen string

4 onions (1 lb), cut into ¼-inch-thick rings

6 plum tomatoes (1¼ lb), quartered lengthwise

2½ lb yellow-fleshed potatoes such as Yukon Gold

½ stick (¼ cup) unsalted butter, softened

Preheat oven to 300°F.

Season shanks with salt and pepper. Toss together onions, tomatoes, and salt and pepper to taste in a 5- to 6-quart ovenproof heavy pot just wide enough to hold shanks in 1 layer. Add shanks and braise, covered, in middle of oven until very tender, about 3 hours.

MAKE MASHED POTATOES AFTER SHANKS HAVE BEEN BRAISING 2¼ HOURS:

Peel potatoes and cut into roughly 2-inch pieces. Cover potatoes with cold salted water by 2 inches in a 4-quart pot and simmer until tender, about 25 minutes. Reserve ½ cup potato cooking water, then drain potatoes in a colander. Return potatoes to pot and add butter and ¼ cup reserved cooking water. Mash until smooth, adding enough of remaining cooking water to reach desired consistency, then season with salt and pepper.

Transfer shanks, onions, and tomatoes to a platter with a slotted spoon. Keep warm, loosely covered with foil. Deglaze pot by boiling braising liquid over high heat, stirring and scraping up any brown bits, until reduced to about 1 cup, about 5 minutes. Season jus with salt and pepper.

Serve shanks, onions, and tomatoes with mashed potatoes and jus.

COOKS' NOTES

• Shanks may be braised 2 days ahead and cooled, uncovered, before being chilled, covered. Reheat shanks and make jus just before serving.

• Potatoes may be cooked and mashed 2 days ahead and cooled, uncovered, before being chilled, covered. Reheat before serving.

SERVES 4

CHEESECAKE VARIETIES ABOUND, but the cheeses used to make them generally are one of the following: cream cheese, farmer cheese, or ricotta. When we specify cream cheese in a recipe, we mean none other than Philadelphia brand. The more expensive artisanal varieties that you'll spy in fancy foods shops won't give you the finished texture that you're after. Farmer cheese, which sounds esoteric but is available at supermarkets, is grainier and drier than cream cheese. It will give you a firmer cake. And, as far as the ricotta is concerned, we use Polly-O; however, unlike the cream-cheese cheesecake recipes, any kind of ricotta will work. If a local Italian market has wonderful fresh ricotta, then by all means use it.

Cheesecake crusts can range from none at all (the cake itself forms a skin while baking) to crumb crusts and full-fledged pastry crusts. We love the different textures and flavors that a good crumb crust imparts. Often Gourmet's food editors use graham crackers, vanilla or chocolate wafers, and gingersnaps.

How do you prevent a cheesecake from cracking? A zillion theories abound, but the most important thing to remember is, do not overbake. We also find it helpful to run a knife around the edge of the cake as soon as it comes out of the oven. The cake will shrink as it cools and, if the side of the cake is stuck to the pan, the surface will split open. Sometimes this happens no matter how painstaking you are. You can camouflage the damage by carefully spreading a thin layer of sour cream onto the chilled cake; leave it in the fridge overnight to set up.

When buying a springform pan, look for one that's marked 24 centimeters. (Depending on the manufacturer, the pans are variously sized as 9 inches or 9½ inches across, but disregard this.) Professional bakers treat their springform pans with T.L.C., and you should, too. Always open a springform on a counter, not in midair, so that it won't warp. (You don't want it to leak.) After you wash it, dry it right away—sour cream will not hide that unmistakable rust taste. We pop ours in a low oven to ensure that they're completely dry.

Transferring a cheesecake from springform to serving plate is an easy matter if you turn the bottom over before filling so that the lip side is down; with the lip out of the way, it's also easier to cut. And speaking of which, one way to ensure clean slices is to use a sharp, thin knife and wipe it off between slices. Dipping the knife repeatedly into hot water can also be effective, but wipe off the knife to keep from adding excess moisture.

—JANE DANIELS LEAR

Three cities of spain cheesecake

SANTA FE'S

THREE CITIES

OF SPAIN

COFFEEHOUSE

(WHICH CLOSED

IN THE 1970s)

CREATED THIS

CREAMY

FAVORITE.

3 (8-oz) packages cream cheese, softened

4 large eggs

2 teaspoons vanilla

1 cup plus 1 tablespoon sugar

Crumb crust (recipe follows)

2 (8-oz) containers sour cream

Preheat oven to 350°F.

Beat cream cheese with an electric mixer until fluffy. Add eggs 1 at a time, beating on low speed, then 1 teaspoon vanilla and 1 cup sugar, beating until incorporated.

Put springform pan with crust in a shallow baking pan (to catch drips). Pour filling into crust, then bake in middle of oven until cake is set 3 inches from edge but center is still slightly wobbly when pan is gently shaken, about 45 minutes. Let stand in baking pan on a rack 5 minutes. Leave oven on.

Stir together sour cream, remaining tablespoon sugar, and remaining teaspoon vanilla. Drop spoonfuls around edge of cake, then spread gently over center, smoothing evenly. Bake cake with topping 10 minutes.

Run a knife around top edge of cake to loosen and cool completely in springform pan on rack (cake will continue to set as it cools). Chill, loosely covered, at least 6 hours. Remove side of pan and transfer cake to a plate. Bring to room temperature before serving.

COOKS' NOTES

• Cheesecake keeps, covered and chilled, 3 days.

• For a delicious ginger cheesecake variation: Add ½ teaspoon ground ginger to crust. For filling, reduce sugar to ¾ cup and pulse in a food processor with ½ cup coarsely chopped crystallized ginger (4 oz) and 1½ tablespoons grated peeled fresh ginger until gingers are finely ground.

MAKES A **9-INCH** CHEESECAKE

Crumb crust

1½ cups finely ground graham crackers or cookies such as chocolate or vanilla wafers or gingersnaps

5 tablespoons unsalted butter, melted

⅓ cup sugar

⅛ teaspoon salt

Special equipment: a 9-inch (24-centimeter) springform pan (see box on page 72)

Stir together all ingredients and press onto bottom and 1 inch up side of buttered springform pan. Fill right away or chill up to 2 hours.

Fireside pizza

EVERYTHING TASTES BETTER when it's made at home—even pizza. We had to be convinced of this, but Michele and Charles Scicolone's pizzas, featured here, did the trick. All you'll require are a few ultra-fresh ingredients, a pizza stone or unglazed "quarry" tiles, and a good hot oven. You'll also need a few hours for the dough to rise twice, but on a lazy Sunday afternoon, with the right company and an assortment of great Italian snacks, this should be no problem.

Port-poached figs with butter-toasted rosemary almonds and prosciutto

1½ lb dried figs, such as Mission

1 cup tawny Port

1 cup water

1 tablespoon sugar

1½ teaspoons black pepper

2 tablespoons unsalted butter

1 lb whole almonds with skins

2 teaspoons chopped fresh rosemary

1 lb thinly sliced prosciutto

Simmer figs, Port, water, sugar, and pepper in a large saucepan, covered, stirring occasionally, until figs are tender, about 15 minutes. Transfer figs with sauce to a serving bowl and cool to room temperature.

Heat butter in a large nonstick skillet over moderately high heat until foam subsides, then toast almonds with rosemary and salt and pepper to taste, stirring, until 1 shade darker, about 5 minutes. Transfer almonds to paper towels to drain and cool.

Serve almonds and prosciutto on separate plates with figs.

COOKS' NOTES

• Almonds may be prepared 1 day ahead and kept in an airtight container at room temperature.

• Figs may be prepared 1 day ahead and kept in their sauce, covered and chilled.

SERVES 8

Greek country salad

1 tablespoon fresh lemon juice

½ teaspoon salt

1 teaspoon honey

⅓ cup extra-virgin olive oil

½ lb escarole (preferably pale inner leaves), chopped (4 cups)

¼ lb tender young mustard greens, trimmed and finely chopped (2 cups)

½ lb dandelion greens, tough stems discarded and leaves cut crosswise into ¼-inch-thick slices (2 cups)

2 oz baby spinach (2 cups)

1 cup watercress sprigs, trimmed

½ cup chopped fresh dill

¼ cup fresh flat-leaf parsley

¼ cup thinly sliced scallion

Whisk together lemon juice, salt, and honey in a large salad bowl, then add oil in a slow stream, whisking.

Add remaining ingredients to dressing and toss to coat. Season with salt and pepper.

SERVES 8

THIS SALAD MIMICS A POPULAR ONE FROM THE GREEK COUNTRYSIDE WITH A FEW WILD GREENS FORAGED FROM THE LAND.

Pizza with garlic and olive oil

OUR PIZZA

RECIPES

EACH MAKE 2

PIZZAS. YOU'LL

NEED TO

ASSEMBLE AND

BAKE ONE

PIZZA AT

A TIME.

2 large garlic cloves, finely chopped

2 tablespoons olive oil

½ teaspoon dried oregano, crumbled

Pinch of dried hot red pepper flakes

Coarse salt to taste

Neopolitan-style pizza dough
(recipe follows)

All-purpose flour for dusting

Special equipment: a pizza stone or 4 to 6 unglazed "quarry" tiles (see box on page 78) and a baker's peel or rimless baking sheet

At least 45 minutes before baking pizza, put pizza stone or "quarry" tiles (arrange tiles close together) on oven rack in lowest position in oven and preheat oven to highest setting (500°– 550°F).

Stir together garlic, oil, oregano, red pepper flakes, and coarse salt in a small bowl.

Pat out 1 ball of dough evenly with your fingers into a 9-inch round, keeping hands flat and lifting and turning dough over several times. (Do not handle dough more than necessary. If dough is sticky, dust lightly with flour.)

Dust baker's peel with flour and carefully transfer dough onto it. Jerk peel once or twice and, if dough is sticking, lift dough and sprinkle flour underneath it, reshaping if necessary. Working quickly, top dough with half of oil mixture, spreading with back of a spoon to within ½ inch of edge.

Line up far edge of peel with far edge of stone or tiles and tilt peel, jerking it gently to start pizza moving. Once edge of pizza touches stone or tiles, carefully pull back peel, completely transferring pizza to stone or tiles (do not move pizza). Bake until dough is crisp and browned, 6

to 7 minutes, then transfer with a metal spatula to a cutting board.

While pizza bakes, pat out second ball of dough and prepare another pizza in same manner. Bake second pizza.

MAKES 2 (9-INCH) PIZZAS

Neopolitan-style pizza dough

IF MAKING

4 (9-INCH)

PIZZAS, YOU'LL

NEED TO MAKE

2 DOUGH

RECIPES. DON'T

DOUBLE THE

RECIPE—

THE DOUGH

WILL BE TOO

UNWIELDY

TO KNEAD.

¾ cup warm water (105° to 115°F)

1½ teaspoons dry active yeast

2 cups unbleached all-purpose flour plus additional for dusting

1 teaspoon salt

Stir together water and yeast until yeast is dissolved. Whisk together flour and salt in a large bowl. Add yeast mixture and stir until a soft dough forms. Knead dough on a lightly floured surface until smooth and elastic, about 10 minutes.

Oil a large bowl (preferably with olive oil) and transfer dough to bowl, turning to coat. Cover bowl with plastic wrap. Let dough rise in a warm place until doubled in bulk, about 1½ hours.

Flatten dough with your hands on a lightly floured surface. Cut dough in half and form 2 balls. Dust tops of balls with flour and cover each with an inverted bowl large enough to allow dough to expand. Let dough rise in a warm place until doubled in bulk, about 1 hour.

COOKS' NOTE

• Dough may be made 1 day ahead (to point of dividing into 2 balls). Wrap balls loosely in plastic wrap and chill in a small sealable plastic bag. Bring dough to room temperature before proceeding.

MAKES DOUGH FOR 2 (9-INCH) PIZZAS

Prosciutto and arugula pizza

Neopolitan-style pizza dough
(recipe on page 76)

All-purpose flour for dusting

1 cup pizza sauce (recipe follows)

¼ lb mozzarella (preferably fresh),
thinly sliced

1 cup small to medium arugula leaves,
tough stems removed

6 very thin slices prosciutto

Special equipment: a pizza stone or 4 to 6
unglazed "quarry" tiles (see box, right) and
a baker's peel or rimless baking sheet

At least 45 minutes before baking pizza, put
pizza stone or "quarry" tiles (arrange tiles close
together) on oven rack in lowest position in oven
and preheat oven to highest setting (500°–550°F).

Pat out 1 ball of dough evenly with your fingers
into a 9-inch round, keeping hands flat and lifting and turning dough over several times. (Do
not handle dough more than necessary. If dough
is sticky, dust lightly with flour.)

Dust baker's peel with flour and carefully transfer
dough onto it. Jerk peel once or twice and,
if dough is sticking, lift dough and sprinkle
flour underneath it, reshaping if necessary.
Working quickly, top dough with half of sauce,
spreading with back of a spoon to within ½ inch
of edge. Arrange half of mozzarella slices evenly
over sauce.

Line up far edge of peel with far edge of stone or
tiles and tilt peel, jerking it gently to start pizza
moving. Once edge of pizza touches stone or
tiles, carefully pull back peel, completely transferring pizza to stone or tiles (do not move
pizza). Bake until dough is crisp and browned, 6
to 7 minutes, then transfer with a metal spatula
to a cutting board. Scatter half of arugula over
pizza and top with half of prosciutto slices.

While pizza bakes, pat out second ball of dough
and prepare another pizza in same manner. Bake
second pizza and top in same manner.

MAKES 2 (9-INCH) PIZZAS

Pizza stones and unglazed "quarry" tiles

THERE'S NOTHING LIKE a pizza, or baking,
stone (along with a hotter-than-Hades oven) to
give your pizza a crisp, well-browned "professional" crust. Thoroughly preheated on an
oven rack set in the lowest position (at least 45
minutes, starting with a cold oven), a stone
enables the dough to warm up quickly and
more evenly than it would in a metal pan.
Because it is made of porous clay, the stone
also absorbs moisture from the dough, pro-
ducing a crisper bottom all the way across and
a wonderful chewy crust around the edge.
(When cleaning, do not use soap! It will be
absorbed by the clay and, in turn, by the pizza.)

Stones are available at cookware shops
and by mail order from The Baker's
Catalogue, (800-827-6836). Unglazed "quarry"
tiles make a good alternative; they can often
be found at the above sources as well as at
many tile stores listed in the Yellow Pages.

Stones or tiles should be seasoned in a
low oven before using. The ones specifically
sold for baking come with manufacturer's
instructions for seasoning; quarry tiles should
be heated once or twice in a 350° F oven for
30 minutes.

—JANE DANIELS LEAR

Pizza sauce

1 (28-oz) can crushed Italian tomatoes in purée (3½ cups)

3 tablespoons olive oil

Simmer crushed tomatoes in purée and oil in a large non-reactive saucepan, uncovered, stirring occasionally, until reduced to about 2½ cups, about 20 minutes. Season with salt and cool to room temperature.

COOKS' NOTE

• Sauce keeps, covered and chilled, 5 days.

MAKES ABOUT 2½ CUPS

Tiramisù

2 tablespoons instant-espresso powder

2 cups boiling water

1 lb mascarpone cheese (2 cups)

¼ cup dark rum

4 oz fine-quality bittersweet chocolate (not unsweetened), finely chopped

4 large egg whites

⅛ teaspoon cream of tartar

1¼ cups sugar

½ cup cold water

60 ladyfingers

Garnish: shaved bittersweet chocolate

Special equipment: a standing electric mixer; a candy thermometer; and 2 (8-inch) glass loaf pans

Stir espresso powder into boiling water, then cool. Whisk together mascarpone, rum, and chocolate in another bowl.

Beat egg whites with cream of tartar and a pinch of salt in large bowl of standing mixer until they just hold stiff peaks.

Meanwhile, bring sugar and cold water to a boil in a small saucepan, stirring until sugar is dissolved. Boil syrup, undisturbed, until it registers 240°F on candy thermometer, then remove from heat and let stand 30 seconds. With mixer running, add hot syrup to whites in a slow stream, beating until mixture is completely cool, about 8 minutes. Add mascarpone mixture and beat until combined well.

Working with 1 ladyfinger at a time, dip one side briefly (do not let soak or ladyfingers will fall apart) into espresso mixture, then transfer to bottom of loaf pan. Line bottom of pan with 9 more dipped ladyfingers in same manner (you will need to halve some ladyfingers to fit). Spread one fourth of mascarpone mixture (about 1½ cups) evenly over ladyfingers, then repeat dipping and layering with another 10 ladyfingers and one fourth mascarpone mixture. Top with another layer of 10 dipped ladyfingers. Make another tiramisù in same manner in second loaf pan with remaining ladyfingers and mascarpone mixture.

Chill tiramisù, loosely covered, at least 6 hours.

COOKS' NOTE

• Tiramisù can be chilled up to 1 day.

SERVES 8

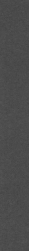

Pancakes for breakfast

EVEN IF YOU'RE NOT a pancake fan, you must try these. We've combined cornmeal and cream cheese for exceptional texture and creamy flavor, then added a warm maple syrup studded with dried fruits. They're reason enough to get out of bed in the morning, but perhaps a refreshing smoothie and decadent slices of ham "frizzled" with a touch of brown sugar and cumin will entice you further. Keep this little menu in mind the next time you have overnight guests.

Pineapple-banana smoothie

2 ripe bananas

4 cups (1-inch cubes) peeled fresh pineapple

½ cup fresh orange juice

½ cup cold water

1 tablespoon fresh lemon juice

2 cups ice cubes

Cut bananas into 1-inch slices. Purée all ingredients in 2 batches in a blender until smooth, transferring to a pitcher. Stir, then serve in ice-filled glasses.

SERVES **4**

Frizzled ham

2½ teaspoons dark brown sugar

½ teaspoon ground cumin

12 thin slices Black Forest ham

Preheat broiler.

Stir together sugar and cumin.

Line each of 12 cups of a lightly oiled ½-cup muffin tin with a slice of ham, gathering and pleating edges decoratively, then sprinkle with sugar mixture. Broil ham 2 to 3 inches from heat until edges are dark brown and crisp, 2 to 3 minutes. Cool in pan on a rack 5 minutes, then transfer ham with tongs onto serving plates.

SERVES **4**

Cornmeal cream cheese pancakes with dried cranberries and apricots in maple syrup

FOR SYRUP

1 cup pure maple syrup

¼ cup dried cranberries

¼ cup chopped dried apricots

2 teaspoons fresh lemon juice

FOR PANCAKES

¾ cup all-purpose flour

½ cup yellow cornmeal

1½ teaspoons baking powder

½ teaspoon baking soda

2 tablespoons sugar

¼ teaspoon salt

⅔ cup spreadable cream cheese in tub (not whipped or block cream cheese)

2 large eggs

¾ cup milk

2 tablespoons unsalted butter, melted

MAKE SYRUP:

Simmer syrup, cranberries, and apricots in a saucepan, uncovered, until fruits are plumped, about 5 minutes. Remove from heat and stir in lemon juice.

MAKE PANCAKES:

Preheat oven to 250°F.

Whisk together flour, cornmeal, baking powder and soda, sugar, and salt. Whisk together cream cheese and eggs in a large bowl, then gradually add milk, whisking until smooth. Add flour mixture and whisk until just combined.

Heat a large griddle over moderate heat until hot enough to make drops of water scatter over its surface, then brush with some butter. Drop tablespoons of batter onto griddle, without crowding, to form 2½-inch cakes. Cook pancakes until golden and puffed, 1 to 2 minutes on each side. Transfer to a baking sheet and keep warm in oven. Make more pancakes in same manner, brushing griddle with some butter between each batch.

Serve pancakes in stacks with syrup.

SERVES 4

Everyone loves pancakes, but some mornings you'd probably rather not find yourself parked in front of a hot griddle. Instead, you might want to prepare our easy French toast the night before. The next morning, simply pop the soaked bread in the oven. By the time the table is set, breakfast will be ready, and you'll be none the worse for wear.

1 (13- to 14-inch-long) loaf of soft-crust supermarket Italian bread

½ stick (¼ cup) unsalted butter, softened

2 large eggs

1⅔ cups whole milk

3 tablespoons sugar

Accompaniment: pure maple syrup

Cut 12 (1-inch-thick) diagonal slices from bread, reserving ends for another use, then generously butter 1 side of each slice. Arrange slices, buttered sides up, in 1 layer in a buttered 13- by 9- by 2-inch glass baking dish, squeezing them slightly to fit if necessary.

Whisk together eggs, milk, and ¼ teaspoon salt until combined well, then pour evenly over bread. Chill, covered, until bread has absorbed all of custard, at least 1 hour and up to 1 day, depending on bread.

Preheat oven to 425°F.

Bring mixture to room temperature and sprinkle bread with sugar. Bake, uncovered, in middle of oven until bread is puffed and top is golden, 20 to 25 minutes. Serve immediately.

SERVES **4** GENEROUSLY

Lasagne supper

WHETHER THE KIDS WANT to have their friends stay for supper or you have weekend guests, it helps to have a substantial menu on hand that will feed a crowd. Lasagne is always a good choice, because it can be made quickly with staples from the pantry and still serve many, usually with leftovers to spare. This menu, perfect for any chilly night, features a meatless lasagne that's lighter than most, but since it has plenty of cheese, it's hearty and warming. We've paired it with some of our favorite autumnal flavors—kabocha squash, pears, and goat cheese.

Roasted kabocha squash soup with pancetta and sage

1 (4-lb) kabocha squash, halved and seeded

1 cup vegetable oil

20 fresh sage leaves plus 1½ teaspoons chopped fresh sage

¼ lb sliced *pancetta*, coarsely chopped (see box, right)

1 tablespoon olive oil

1 large onion, chopped

2 garlic cloves, minced

3½ cups chicken broth

3½ cups water

1 tablespoon red-wine vinegar

Special equipment: deep-fat thermometer

ROAST SQUASH:

Preheat oven to 400°F.

Roast squash, cut sides down, in an oiled roasting pan in middle of oven until tender, about 1 hour. When cool enough to handle, scrape flesh from skin.

FRY SAGE LEAVES WHILE SQUASH ROASTS:

Heat vegetable oil in a deep small saucepan until it registers 365°F on a deep-fat thermometer. Fry sage leaves in 3 batches until crisp, 3 to 5 seconds. Transfer with a slotted spoon to paper towels to drain.

COOK PANCETTA AND MAKE SOUP:

Cook *pancetta* in a 4-quart heavy pot over moderate heat, stirring, until browned. Transfer *pancetta* with slotted spoon to paper towels to drain.

Add olive oil to *pancetta* fat remaining in pot, then cook onion, stirring, until softened. Add garlic and chopped sage and cook, stirring, until fragrant, about 1 minute. Add squash, broth, and water and simmer 20 minutes (to blend flavors).

Purée soup in batches in a blender, transferring to a bowl. (Use caution when blending hot liquids.) Return soup to pot and reheat. If necessary, thin to desired consistency with additional water. Stir in vinegar and salt and pepper to taste.

Serve soup sprinkled with *pancetta* and fried sage leaves.

COOKS' NOTE

• Soup can be made 3 days ahead and chilled, covered.

SERVES 8 (MAKES ABOUT 11 CUPS)

Pancetta

WHEN WE USED PANCETTA—Italian bacon that's been salt-cured but not smoked—in our squash soup, we were reminded of how its wonderful flavor resonates through a dish. Pancetta is at its most voluptuous in *spaghetti alla carbonara*, but you can use it any time you want a hammy-but-not-smoky flavor—in a minestrone, say, or with winter greens. Look for *pancetta* at Italian markets and specialty foods shops; the person behind the meat counter will slice it paper-thin for you. Pancetta keeps, tightly wrapped, in the fridge for about a week or frozen for up to three months.

—JANE DANIELS LEAR

Tomato and mozzarella lasagne

FOR SAUCE

3 onions, chopped

1 tablespoon unsalted butter

2 tablespoons olive oil

½ teaspoon dried oregano, crumbled

½ teaspoon dried thyme

6 garlic cloves, minced

3 (28- to 32-oz) cans crushed tomatoes in thick purée

1 cup chopped fresh flat-leaf parsley

¼ cup fresh orange juice

FOR LASAGNE

18 (7- by 3½-inch) sheets dry no-boil lasagne (1 lb)

2½ lb fresh mozzarella (smoked or plain), chilled and coarsely grated (6 cups)

1 cup freshly grated parmesan

MAKE SAUCE:

Cook onion in butter and oil with oregano, thyme, and salt and pepper to taste in a 4-quart saucepan over moderate heat, stirring, until onion is softened. Add garlic and cook, stirring, 1 minute. Add tomatoes in purée and simmer, uncovered, stirring occasionally, until slightly thickened, about 18 minutes. Remove from heat and stir in parsley, orange juice, and salt and pepper to taste.

ASSEMBLE LASAGNE:

Preheat oven to 375°F and butter 2 (13- by 9-inch) baking dishes.

Soak lasagne sheets in hot water to cover by 1 inch until softened and flexible, about 20 minutes.

Spread 1½ cups sauce in each baking dish and top sauce in each dish with 3 drained pasta sheets, overlapping if necessary. Sprinkle 1 cup mozzarella and ¼ cup parmesan evenly in each dish. Top with 3 drained pasta sheets per dish, overlapping if necessary. Repeat layering with 1 cup mozzarella, ¼ cup parmesan, 1½ cups sauce, and 3 drained pasta sheets in each dish. Finish by topping each with 1½ cups sauce. (You will have leftover sauce and mozzarella.)

Bake lasagne, covered with foil, in middle of oven 30 minutes. Remove foil and sprinkle evenly with remaining 2 cups mozzarella. Bake until bubbling and cheese is melted, about 10 minutes more.

Serve lasagne with some of remaining sauce, reheated.

COOKS' NOTES

• Sauce may be made 3 days ahead and chilled, covered.

• You can assemble and bake lasagne up to point of adding last layer of mozzarella 1 day ahead. Cool completely, then chill, covered. Bring to room temperature before reheating with final layer of mozzarella, covered, in a 375°F oven until hot, 20 to 30 minutes.

SERVES 8 (WITH LEFTOVERS)

Pear, pine nut, and watercress salad

1½ tablespoons Sherry vinegar

1 teaspoon Dijon mustard

6½ tablespoons olive oil

½ cup pine nuts

2 ripe Anjou or Bosc pears

6 cups tender watercress sprigs (½ lb)

3 Belgian endives, cut crosswise
into 1-inch-wide slices

Whisk together vinegar, mustard, and salt and pepper to taste. Add 6 tablespoons oil in a slow stream, whisking until emulsified.

Heat remaining ½ tablespoon oil in a heavy skillet over moderate heat until hot but not smoking, then toast nuts with salt to taste, stirring occasionally, until golden brown, about 5 minutes. Transfer to paper towels to drain.

Quarter pears lengthwise and core. Cut pears crosswise into ¼-inch-thick slices, then toss with watercress, endive, half of nuts, and enough dressing to coat. Season with salt and pepper and top with remaining nuts.

SERVES **8**

Orange star-anise sorbet

⅓ cup water

½ cup sugar

2 whole star anise

4 cups fresh orange juice

Special equipment: an ice-cream maker

Boil water, sugar, and star anise in a small saucepan, stirring until sugar is dissolved. Remove saucepan from heat and let syrup steep 30 minutes.

Pour syrup through a sieve, then stir together with juice and chill until cold.

Freeze in an ice-cream maker. Transfer to an airtight container and put in freezer to harden.

COOKS' NOTE

• Sorbet keeps 1 week.

SERVES **8**

SOMEBODY'S TURNING

the big 4-0, or its graduation
time, or the Oscars are on
again and they're no fun to
watch alone. For all those
times when there's reason
enough to throw a small
party at home, here is a collection of foolproof menus
you can trust. Though all of
the following parties are
relaxed in nature, each is
filled with wonderful flavors
and the right amount of style
to make it known that this is
no ordinary occasion.

Super bowl party

WATCHING THE SUPER BOWL is a
time-honored tradition—even those who
haven't seen a single game in the regular
season gather to catch the big one on TV.
Rather than serving your trophy-winning
chili (the usual standby) again, why not try
something a little different this year?
Pozole rojo, a hearty pork and hominy stew
from Mexico, is just as sure to please a
crowd, as are rosy-hued *pomegranitas* and
luscious cinnamon-coffee flan. A few
unadventurous sports fans may be
apprehensive at first, but they'll soon
come around.

Pomegranitas

1 cup fresh pomegranate juice
(from 2 pomegranates) or 1½ cups
cranberry juice cocktail

1 cup white tequila

¼ cup triple sec

4 cups ice cubes

Garnish: orange slices

Stir together juice, tequila, and triple sec in a large (4-cup) glass measure, then pour over ice in a pitcher. Stir until cold and serve, straining out ice.

COOKS' NOTE

• To juice pomegranates, roll them firmly against a work surface, then poke a hole through the skin with the tip of a sharp knife and squeeze out juice.

SERVES 8

Cheese and red bell pepper quesadillas

1 large onion, chopped

1 red bell pepper, seeded and chopped

1½ tablespoons olive oil

½ teaspoon ground cumin

8 (7- to 8-inch) flour tortillas

8 oz coarsely grated Pepper Jack cheese (2 cups)

Special equipment: 2 (17- by 14-inch) heavy-duty baking sheets

Preheat oven to 450°F.

Cook onion and bell pepper in oil in a 12-inch skillet over moderate heat, stirring occasionally, until softened, 5 to 7 minutes. Stir in cumin and salt and pepper to taste and cook mixture, stirring, 1 minute.

Arrange 4 tortillas on an ungreased baking sheet and top evenly with bell pepper mixture. Sprinkle evenly with cheese, then top with remaining 4 tortillas. Put second baking sheet on top of quesadillas as a weight. Bake in middle of oven until cheese is bubbling and tortillas are lightly browned, 10 to 12 minutes. Remove top baking sheet and transfer quesadillas to a cutting board. Cut each into 6 wedges.

SERVES 8

Salsa ranchera

1 medium white onion, quartered

3 lb medium tomatoes, cored

½ cup olive oil

1 fresh *serrano* chile, chopped, including seeds

½ cup chopped fresh cilantro

3 tablespoons red-wine vinegar

Accompaniment: corn tortilla chips

Preheat oven to 400°F.

Arrange 2 onion quarters and 2 pounds tomatoes in a small roasting pan and drizzle with ¼ cup oil. Arrange remaining 1 pound tomatoes in another small roasting pan and drizzle with remaining ¼ cup oil. Bake both pans of tomatoes in upper and lower thirds of oven, switching position of pans after 45 minutes, until browned, about 1½ hours total. Remove pan with more tomatoes and continue baking other pan until tomatoes are blackened, about 30 minutes more.

Transfer all roasted tomatoes (do not peel) and onions with a slotted spoon to a food processor, discarding liquid in pans. (If your processor is small, do this in 2 batches.) Pulse until coarsely chopped. (Alternatively, you can chop with an immersion blender in a deep container.) Chop remaining 2 onion quarters and stir together with tomato mixture, chile, cilantro, and vinegar. Season with salt and chill, covered, at least 8 hours to blend flavors. Bring to room temperature before serving.

COOKS' NOTE

• Salsa keeps, covered and chilled, 3 days.

MAKES ABOUT 4 CUPS
Photo on page 90

Pozole rojo
Pork and hominy stew with red chiles

1 large head garlic

12 cups water

4 cups chicken broth

4 lb country-style pork ribs

1 teaspoon dried oregano (preferably Mexican), crumbled

2 oz dried New Mexico red chiles, stems discarded

1½ cups boiling-hot water

¼ large white onion, cut into large pieces

3 teaspoons salt

2 (30-oz) cans white hominy (preferably Bush's Best), rinsed and drained

8 corn tortillas

1½ cups vegetable oil

Accompaniments: diced avocado, thinly sliced iceberg or romaine lettuce, chopped white onion, diced radishes, lime wedges, dried oregano, and dried hot red pepper flakes

Peel garlic cloves and reserve 2 for chile sauce, then slice remaining garlic. Bring water, broth, sliced garlic, and pork just to a boil in a 7- to 8-quart heavy pot. Skim surface and add oregano. Gently simmer pork, uncovered, until tender, about 1½ hours.

While pork simmers, soak chiles in boiling-hot water in a bowl, turning them occasionally, 30 minutes. Purée chiles and soaking liquid, onion, reserved garlic, and 2 teaspoons salt in a blender until smooth.

Transfer pork with tongs to a cutting board and reserve broth mixture. Shred pork with 2 forks and discard bones. Return pork to broth mixture and add red chile sauce, hominy, and remaining teaspoon salt. Simmer pozole 30 minutes and, if necessary, season with salt.

While pork simmers, stack tortillas and halve. Cut halves crosswise into thin strips. Heat ½ inch oil in a 10-inch skillet until hot but not smoking, then fry tortilla strips in 3 or 4 batches, stirring occasionally, until golden, 1 to 2 minutes, transferring them with a slotted spoon to brown paper or paper towels to drain, then to a bowl.

Serve pozole with tortilla strips.

COOKS' NOTES

• Pozole may be made 2 days ahead and chilled, covered.

• Strips may be made 1 day ahead and kept in an airtight container at room temperature.

SERVES **8**

Cinnamon-coffee flan

1½ cups sugar

4 cups half-and-half

2 cinnamon sticks, halved lengthwise

1 (4- by 1-inch) strip orange zest

4 teaspoons instant-espresso powder

4 large whole eggs

4 large egg yolks

Preheat oven to 350°F.

Cook 1 cup sugar in a dry 10-inch nonstick skillet over moderate heat, swirling pan (to help sugar melt evenly), until sugar is melted to a deep golden caramel, 8 to 10 minutes. Immediately pour into a 9- by 2-inch round cake pan, tilting to coat bottom and sides evenly, then let cool.

Bring half-and-half, cinnamon sticks, zest, and espresso powder to a simmer in a 3-quart heavy saucepan, stirring occasionally. Remove from heat and let stand, covered, 20 minutes. Return to a simmer, then discard cinnamon sticks and zest.

Whisk together eggs, yolks, remaining ½ cup sugar, and a pinch of salt, then gradually add hot half-and-half mixture, whisking. Pour into coated cake pan and bake in a hot water bath in middle of oven until set but still trembling slightly in center, 45 to 50 minutes. (Custard will continue to set as it cools.) Cool custard on a rack 30 minutes, then chill, covered, until cold, at least 2 hours.

Run a knife around inside edge of pan and invert custard onto a serving platter with a lip (to hold caramel sauce).

COOKS' NOTE

• Flan may be chilled (in cake pan) up to 2 days.

SERVES **8**

An engagement party

A RECENT ENGAGEMENT calls for serious celebrating with Champagne—lots of it—and a lovely party that'll let the future bride and groom know how thrilled you are for them. The menu offers a clever mix of both the uncommon and luxurious (piquillo peppers, sablefish, and naturally, Champagne) and the more familiar and comforting (pork loin, spinach, even mashed potatoes) for a perfect union of flavors. Such a combination calls for a toast.

Champagne cocktails

THIS COCKTAIL
COMES FROM
THE MONKEY
BAR IN NEW
YORK CITY.

1 oz Orange Muscat dessert wine
(2 tablespoons) such as Andrew Quady
Essensia

1¼ cups chilled dry Champagne such
as Moët & Chandon Brut '90

Garnish: orange slices

Combine wine and Champagne in a pitcher and
divide between 2 Champagne coupes.

MAKES 2 DRINKS

Grapefruit coolers

9 cups fresh red grapefruit juice
(2¼ qt; from about 6 grapefruits)

3 cups seltzer or club soda

Garnish: fresh mint sprigs

Stir together juice and seltzer in a pitcher half-
filled with ice cubes.

MAKES ABOUT 12 CUPS

Mi rosa

BEAUTIFUL AND
DELICIOUS, THIS
CHAMPAGNE
COCKTAIL FROM
BOUDROS IN
SAN ANTONIO
IS IDEAL FOR
ANY SPECIAL
OCCASION.

¼ cup raspberries, rinsed and drained

1 oz tequila (2 tablespoons)

1 teaspoon sugar

6 tablespoons fresh orange juice

6 tablespoons chilled Champagne or
sparkling wine

Garnish: short-stemmed rosebud

Blend raspberries, tequila, and sugar in a blender
until smooth, then force through a fine sieve into
a small bowl.

Stir together orange juice and Champagne in a
Champagne flute, then add shaved ice to within
½ inch of rim. Carefully spoon raspberry mixture over ice.

COOKS' NOTE

• We recommend making the purée in batches if
you plan on serving several drinks at once.
Simply multiply the raspberries, tequila, and
sugar by the number you're serving.

MAKES 1 DRINK

Mi rosa, left; Champagne cocktail, right.

Piquillo pepper mousse with pita chips

2 (7- to 8-oz) jars piquillo peppers or roasted red peppers, drained and seeded

3 tablespoons chopped fresh basil

1 garlic clove, smashed

1½ teaspoons fresh lemon juice

1 teaspoon salt

1 teaspoon unflavored gelatin

2 tablespoons water

⅔ cup heavy cream

4 (6-inch) pita pockets, halved horizontally

¼ cup extra-virgin olive oil

Purée peppers, basil, garlic, lemon juice, and salt in a blender or food processor until smooth, then transfer to a bowl.

Sprinkle gelatin over water in a small saucepan and let stand 1 minute to soften. Heat over low heat, stirring, until gelatin is dissolved, 1 to 2 minutes. Remove from heat and whisk ¼ cup purée into gelatin, then fold gelatin mixture into remaining purée.

Beat cream with an electric mixer until it just holds soft peaks. Fold into purée gently but thoroughly, then spoon into a serving bowl. Chill, covered, until firm, at least 2 hours.

PREPARE PITA CHIPS WHILE MOUSSE CHILLS:
Preheat oven to 350°F.

Cut each pita half into 6 wedges. Brush cut sides of wedges with oil and season with salt and pepper, then arrange in 1 layer in 2 ungreased shallow baking pans. Bake in upper and lower thirds of oven, switching pans halfway through baking, until crisp, about 10 minutes. Cool in pans on racks.

Serve mousse with pita chips.

COOKS' NOTES

• Mousse may be chilled up to 2 days.

• Pita chips can be made 2 days ahead and kept in an airtight container at room temperature.

SERVES 12 TO 16

Smoked sablefish canapés

2 small sweet onions such as Vidalia

1 stick (½ cup) unsalted butter, softened

¼ cup bottled horseradish, drained

2 tablespoons chopped fresh dill

8 slices firm pumpernickel bread, trimmed to 3½-inch squares

½ lb sliced moist smoked sablefish or other smoked fish such as whitefish, trout, or salmon, cut into 1-inch pieces

½ English cucumber, halved lengthwise and cut crosswise into 32 thin slices

Garnish: 32 small dill sprigs

Grate enough of 1 onion to measure 1 tablespoon, reserving remainder for another use, then mash together with butter, horseradish, chopped dill, and salt and pepper to taste in a small bowl.

Quarter remaining whole onion and cut lengthwise into 32 thin slices. Spread 1 side of bread squares with half of horseradish butter. Cut each diagonally into 4 triangles, then top each triangle with 1 slice of onion. Dab a tiny bit of butter on onion, then top with 1 piece of fish and another dab of butter. Top with 1 cucumber slice, a dab of butter, and 1 sprig of dill.

- Horseradish butter can be made 1 day ahead and chilled, covered. Soften before using.

- Canapés can be assembled 1 hour ahead and covered with damp paper towels and plastic wrap.

MAKES 32 HORS D'OEUVRES

Apricot-stuffed pork loin

2 tablespoons curry powder
(preferably Madras)

2 teaspoons salt

1 teaspoon black pepper

3 tablespoons unsalted butter

2 large onions, chopped (3 cups)

12 oz dried apricots, coarsely chopped (2 cups)

2 cups water

2 (4-lb) boneless pork loins, tied by a butcher

Stir together 1 tablespoon curry powder, salt, and pepper in a small bowl.

Heat butter in a 12-inch skillet over moderate heat until foam subsides, then cook onions, stirring occasionally, until softened, 5 to 7 minutes. Stir in apricots and remaining tablespoon curry powder and cook 1 minute. Add 1 cup water and simmer, stirring occasionally, until liquid is absorbed, about 5 minutes. Remove from heat and season with salt and pepper. Cool.

Preheat oven to 350°F.

Working with 1 pork loin at a time, cut a horizontal 1½-inch-wide slit through center of loin from end to end with a long thin-bladed knife. Then cut a ½-inch-wide slit through meat perpendicular to first slit. (This forms a cross, wider horizontally than vertically, to make a hole through pork loin.) Cut remaining pork loin in same manner. Stuff each loin with one fourth of apricot mixture, pushing filling into meat from both ends with the handle of a wooden spoon. Pat meat dry and rub with curry powder mixture, then transfer loins to a large roasting pan.

Roast meat, fat sides up, in middle of oven until it registers 155°F on an instant-read thermometer inserted 2 inches into center of meat, 1¼ to 1½ hours. Transfer loins to a carving board and let stand, loosely tented with foil, 15 minutes.

While meat stands, skim off most of fat from roasting pan, then add remaining cup water and deglaze by boiling over high heat, stirring and scraping up brown bits. Transfer to a saucepan with remaining apricot mixture and any juices that have accumulated on carving board. Simmer over moderate heat, stirring occasionally, 5 minutes.

Slice pork loins, removing strings, and serve with sauce.

COOKS' NOTE

- Apricot mixture can be made 1 day ahead and chilled, covered.

SERVES 12 TO 16

Photo on page 98

Baby spinach and mint salad

1½ lb baby spinach

3 cups whole fresh mint leaves
(from 3 bunches)

1 tablespoon coarse-grained mustard

2 tablespoons cider vinegar

1½ teaspoons pure maple syrup

⅓ cup olive oil

Toss together spinach and mint in a large bowl.

Whisk together mustard, vinegar, and syrup, then whisk in oil until well blended. Season with salt and pepper and toss salad with dressing.

COOKS' NOTES
• Spinach and mint may be washed and spun dry 1 day ahead and chilled in sealable plastic bags lined with paper towels.

• Dressing may be made 1 day ahead and chilled, covered. Bring to room temperature before serving.

SERVES 12 TO 16

Parsnip-potato mash

6 lb Yukon Gold potatoes, peeled and each cut into 8 pieces

3 lb parsnips, peeled and cut into 1-inch pieces

2 tablespoons kosher salt

1 stick (½ cup) unsalted butter

Garnish: chopped chives

Cover potatoes and parsnips with cold water by 1 inch in a 7- to 8-quart pot and add kosher salt. Simmer until tender, about 30 minutes. Reserve 2½ cups cooking liquid, then drain vegetables. Mash vegetables, stirring in butter, reserved cooking liquid, and salt and pepper to taste.

SERVES 12 TO 16

Chocolate hazelnut ice-cream cakes

3 (5⅓-oz) boxes fine-quality shortbread

10 oz hazelnuts (2½ cups), toasted and skinned (see procedure on page 179)

3 pints superpremium chocolate ice cream, softened

2 pints heavy cream

⅓ cup confectioners sugar

2 tablespoons hazelnut liqueur such as Frangelico

1½ teaspoons vanilla

Garnish: chocolate shavings

Line 2 (9- by 5-inch) loaf pans with plastic wrap, letting wrap hang over long sides by 2 inches.

Pulse half of shortbread and half of nuts in a food processor until nuts are finely chopped. Pulse remaining shortbread and nuts in same manner. (You should have about 6 cups crumb mixture.)

Spread 1 cup ice cream evenly into 1 loaf pan and sprinkle with 1 cup crumb mixture, pressing down gently. Repeat layering ice cream and crumb mixture 2 more times. Assemble another ice cream cake in second pan in same manner. Cover with overhanging plastic wrap and freeze until firm, 3 to 4 hours.

Beat cream with confectioners sugar, liqueur, and vanilla in a bowl with an electric mixer until it just holds stiff peaks. Unmold ice cream cakes 1 at a time: Invert onto a baking sheet and press a hot damp kitchen towel on bottom of pan 30 seconds, then remove pan and plastic wrap. Frost cakes with whipped cream and freeze until firm, at least 30 minutes.

Cut into ½-inch-thick slices before serving.

COOKS' NOTE

• Frosted cakes can be frozen, wrapped well in plastic wrap, up to 4 days. Unwrap cakes and soften in refrigerator 20 minutes before cutting.

SERVES 12 TO 16

Oscar night party

ALTHOUGH YOU MAY NOT have access to Harry Winston diamonds or Vera Wang couture, you still can host your own little gala Oscars party with dazzling hors d'oeuvres and festive drinks. You'll want to set out as many room-temperature snacks as possible beforehand, and enlist a guest to pour the cocktails—this will ensure a constant flow of nibbles and drink while you bring out the hot hors d'oeuvres. Most important, have all your platters, utensils, garnishes, and accompaniments ready to go, so that you're not scrambling to find them at the last minute.

Martinis

3 oz gin (6 tablespoons)

Splash of dry vermouth

Garnish: lemon twists

Combine gin and vermouth in a cocktail shaker filled halfway with ice and shake well. Strain into 2 chilled Martini glasses.

MAKES **2** DRINKS

Cranberry-lime coolers

5 cups chilled cranberry juice cocktail

¼ cup fresh lime juice

4 cups chilled seltzer

Garnish: lime wedges

Stir together cranberry juice, lime juice, and seltzer and serve over ice.

MAKES ABOUT **8** CUPS

Spiced sherry

2 cups cream Sherry

2 whole cloves

1 whole nutmeg, cracked with a mortar and pestle

1 (3-inch) cinnamon stick

1 (4- by 1-inch) piece lemon zest

Combine all ingredients in a 1-quart glass jar. Cover and let stand at room temperature 1 week. Strain and serve over ice, if desired.

COOKS' NOTE

• Strained spiced Sherry keeps 1 month at room temperature, covered.

MAKES **2** CUPS

ALTHOUGH OUR COCKTAIL parties offer recipes for making specific drinks, they'll require setting up a bar with **the basics:**

- BOURBON
- GIN
- RUM
- TEQUILA
- VERMOUTH (DRY AND SWEET)
- VODKA
- WHISKEY/SCOTCH

You'll also want to make certain that you have enough **mixers** and **non-alcoholic options:**

- CLUB SODA
- COLA
- GINGER ALE
- JUICES (CRANBERRY, ORANGE, TOMATO)
- SELTZER OR OTHER SPARKLING WATER
- TONIC

Of course, you'll need a few **condiments:**

- ANGOSTURA BITTERS
- GRENADINE
- GROUND BLACK PEPPER
- HORSERADISH
- ROSE'S LIME JUICE
- SUPERFINE SUGAR
- TABASCO
- WORCESTERSHIRE SAUCE

And, since any well-made drink, alcoholic or not, deserves a good **garnish:**

- COCKTAIL ONIONS
- LEMONS AND LIMES
- MARASCHINO CHERRIES
- PIMIENTO-STUFFED OLIVES
- ROCK SALT

Perhaps as important as the drinks themselves are the necessary **accoutrements:**

- BAR SPOON
- BOTTLE/CAN OPENER
- COCKTAIL SHAKER AND STRAINER
- CORKSCREW
- ICE BUCKET AND TONGS
- JIGGER

Glassware is equally significant. A reliable double old-fashioned glass will serve most mixed-drink purposes, although Martinis, Cosmopolitans, and the like call for stemmed cocktail glasses. Wineglasses are a straightforward choice when serving wine, although you may wish to serve it in small tumblers, as the French do. Champagne, however, should always be served in flutes. It's wise to stock up on extra glasses whenever you're entertaining, as guests invariably lose track of the ones they start out with.

Finally, if there's one thing you can never have too much of, it's **ice.** Fill ice buckets just before guests arrive and keep spare bags in the freezer. For a large crowd, consider stashing a backup supply in a cooler.

Skewered shrimp with prosciutto and tarragon

Olive oil for brushing

16 to 24 fresh whole tarragon leaves

1 lb large shrimp (16 to 24), shelled and deveined

¼ lb thinly sliced prosciutto, cut lengthwise into 16 to 24 strips

Special equipment: 16 to 24 (8-inch) bamboo skewers

Preheat broiler.

Line a shallow baking pan with aluminum foil and lightly brush with oil.

Place 1 tarragon leaf on each shrimp and wrap 1 piece of prosciutto around each shrimp. Thread each shrimp lengthwise onto a skewer near pointed end. Arrange 6 skewers in a row along a short end of baking pan so blunt ends of skewers point toward middle of pan. Cover exposed portions of skewers with a piece of oiled foil (don't cover shrimp). Arrange another row of skewers over foil. Continue adding rows of skewers and layers of foil, making sure exposed skewer ends of last row of skewers are covered with foil. Brush shrimp with oil.

Broil shrimp 4 to 6 inches from heat until just cooked through, about 4 minutes.

SERVES **8**

Spicy pork shu mei

½ lb ground pork (not lean)

4 scallions, finely chopped, plus 1 tablespoon finely chopped scallion

1 teaspoon grated peeled fresh ginger

3 tablespoons mirin (Japanese sweet rice wine)

½ teaspoon salt

4 soft-leaf lettuce leaves

30 round fresh won ton or gyoza wrappers

24 fresh whole cilantro leaves

2 tablespoons soy sauce

1 teaspoon unseasoned rice vinegar

1 teaspoon toasted sesame oil

Special equipment: a 3-inch round cookie cutter

Mix together pork, 4 chopped scallions, ginger, 1 tablespoon mirin, and salt. Oil a steamer rack and line with lettuce leaves.

Cut wrappers into 3-inch rounds, discarding excess dough. Working with 1 wrapper at a time in the palm of your hand and keeping remaining wrappers covered with plastic wrap, mound 1 teaspoon pork filling in center. Cup hand and press wrapper against filling, forming an open sack. Arrange dumplings as formed in 1 layer on steamer rack.

Steam dumplings over boiling water until filling is cooked through, about 10 minutes. Transfer to a serving plate and top each with 1 cilantro leaf.

Stir together remaining 2 tablespoons mirin, remaining tablespoon scallion, soy sauce, vinegar, and sesame oil in a small bowl and serve with hot dumplings.

SERVES **8**

Leek and potato keftédes

1 large boiling potato (8 oz), peeled and cut into eight pieces

1 lb leeks (white and pale green parts only), trimmed and chopped

2 large eggs, lightly beaten

¼ cup plain dried bread crumbs

About ⅓ cup olive oil for frying

Accompaniment: lemon wedges

Cover potato with cold salted water by 1 inch, then simmer until just tender, 15 to 20 minutes. Drain, then transfer to a bowl and mash.

Cook leeks in a large pot of boiling salted water 3 minutes, then drain. Stir into potato with eggs, bread crumbs, and salt and pepper to taste.

Preheat oven to 200°F.

Heat 3 tablespoons oil in a 10-inch heavy skillet over moderate heat until hot but not smoking, then drop about 8 (1-tablespoon) measures pota- to mixture into oil. Fry fritters, turning once, until golden brown, about 4 minutes. Drain keftédes on paper towels, then transfer to a baking sheet and keep warm in oven. Cook more fritters in same manner, adding more oil as needed.

SERVES 8

Mustard-seed cheddar sticks

¾ stick (6 tablespoons) unsalted butter, cut into bits

¾ cup all-purpose flour

1 tablespoon kosher salt

⅛ teaspoon cayenne

1 cup grated sharp white Cheddar (4 oz)

2 teaspoons mustard seeds

Preheat oven to 400°F.

Pulse butter, flour, 1 teaspoon kosher salt, and cayenne in a food processor until mixture resem- bles coarse meal. Add Cheddar and pulse until mixture forms a dough. Form dough into a disk. Chill dough, wrapped in plastic wrap, until firm, at least 30 minutes.

Roll out dough into a 16- by 4-inch rectangle (about ¼ inch thick) on a lightly floured surface with a lightly floured rolling pin. Trim edges and lightly brush rectangle with water. Sprinkle with mustard seeds and remaining 2 teaspoons salt, then gently roll pin over dough to make seeds and salt adhere.

Cut rectangle crosswise into roughly ⅓-inch- wide sticks with a sharp long knife and transfer with a spatula to a parchment-lined baking sheet, arranging about ¾ inch apart. Bake in middle of oven until golden, about 10 minutes, then transfer to a rack to cool.

COOKS' NOTES

• Dough may be chilled up to 2 days.

• Cheddar sticks may be kept in an airtight con- tainer at cool room temperature 1 week, or frozen 1 month.

MAKES ABOUT 45 STICKS

Photo on page 101

Cucumber caviar canapés

1 English cucumber, cut diagonally
into 8 (⅛-inch-thick) slices

¾ cup sour cream

7 oz caviar

Serve cucumber slices topped with sour cream
and caviar.

COOKS' NOTES

• We used osetra caviar for this hors d'oeuvre,
but feel free to substitute your favorite.

• Any leftover caviar can be used to brighten up a
number of dishes, from scrambled eggs to pasta.

SERVES **8**

Photo on page 100

Curried chicken liver pâté

1 onion, thinly sliced

2¼ sticks (1 cup plus 2 tablespoons)
unsalted butter, cut into 1-tablespoon
pieces

1 lb chicken livers, trimmed and rinsed

2 teaspoons curry powder

2 teaspoons paprika

1¼ teaspoons salt, or to taste

½ teaspoon black pepper

3 tablespoons brandy

Accompaniment: baguette slices oven-
toasted with olive oil, salt, and pepper

Special equipment: a 3½-cup ceramic terrine

Cook onion in 4 tablespoons butter in a large
heavy skillet over moderate heat, stirring, until
softened. Add livers, curry powder, paprika, salt,
and pepper and cook, covered, over moderately
low heat, stirring occasionally, until livers are
barely pink inside, about 10 minutes. Remove
from heat and add brandy.

Purée warm mixture in a food processor with
remaining butter until smooth, then pour into
terrine. Chill, surface of pâté covered with plastic
wrap, until firm, at least 3 hours.

COOKS' NOTE

• Pâté is best the day after it's made. It keeps,
covered and chilled, 1 week.

MAKES ABOUT **3½** CUPS

Meringue kisses

2 large egg whites

½ cup sugar

Accompaniment: lemon curd (recipe follows)

Preheat oven to 200°F and butter and flour a large baking sheet, knocking off excess flour.

Beat whites in a bowl with an electric mixer until they just hold soft peaks. Gradually add sugar, beating, and beat until meringue holds stiff, glossy peaks.

Drop heaping teaspoons (not measuring spoons) of meringue about 1 inch apart onto baking sheet and bake in middle of oven 45 minutes. Turn oven off and leave meringues in oven 1 hour more. Transfer meringues with a metal spatula to a rack to cool completely.

COOKS' NOTE

• Meringue kisses keep in an airtight container at room temperature 5 days.

MAKES ABOUT 24

Lemon curd

3 lemons

¾ cup sugar

2 large eggs

1 stick (½ cup) unsalted butter, cut into 4 pieces

Finely grate enough zest from lemons to measure 2 teaspoons and squeeze enough juice to measure ½ cup. Whisk together zest, juice, sugar, and eggs in a metal bowl, then add butter.

Set bowl over a saucepan of simmering water and cook, whisking occasionally, until curd is thickened and smooth, about 20 minutes. Serve warm or chilled.

COOKS' NOTE

• Lemon curd keeps 3 days, chilled and its surface covered with plastic wrap.

MAKES ABOUT 1⅔ CUPS

Come meet the baby

THERE'S NO BETTER REASON

to throw a party than to introduce the

newest little member of the family. This

get-together must be especially easy, since

a baby is handful enough. Nothing fancy,

just good homey foods that lend them-

selves well to buffet-style entertaining.

And while not too precious or overdone,

our blossom-topped cupakes are never-

theless awfully adorable, in keeping with

the spirit of this afternoon's event.

Sparkling strawberry-mint lemonade

WE LOVE HOW

ATLANTA'S

FOUR SEASONS

HOTEL ADDS

SPARKLING

WATER

TO THEIR

LEMONADE

FOR EXTRA

PIZZAZZ.

1 cup water

2 cups sugar

1¼ lb strawberries (1¼ pints), coarsely chopped

¼ cup packed fresh mint

2 cups fresh lemon juice (10 to 12 large lemons)

1 to 1½ qt chilled sparkling water

Garnish: lemon slices

Simmer water and 1 cup sugar in a small saucepan, stirring until sugar is dissolved. Cool syrup to room temperature.

Purée berries with syrup, mint, lemon juice, and remaining cup sugar in a blender and pour purée through a sieve into a 3-quart pitcher.

Stir in sparkling water to taste and serve over ice.

COOKS' NOTE

• Lemonade (before adding sparkling water) can be made 1 day ahead and chilled, covered.

MAKES ABOUT 2½ QUARTS

Olive-stuffed red pepper wedges

3 large red bell peppers, each cut into 6 wedges and each wedge halved crosswise

2 cups fresh fine bread crumbs (preferably from a baguette)

3 tablespoons *tapenade* (black olive paste)

2 tablespoons finely chopped fresh flat-leaf parsley

1 garlic clove, minced

¼ cup extra-virgin olive oil

Preheat oven to 375°F.

Arrange bell pepper wedges in 1 layer in a lightly oiled large shallow (1-inch-deep) baking pan and season with salt and pepper. Stir together remaining ingredients and divide among wedges, about 1 rounded teaspoon per wedge.

Bake in middle of oven, covered, 20 minutes, then uncover and bake until peppers are slightly softened but still hold their shape, about 10 minutes more. Cool in pan on a rack. Serve warm or at room temperature.

SERVES 10 TO 12

Cheese strudels

1 (15-oz) container whole-milk ricotta

⅓ cup freshly grated parmesan

1 large egg, lightly beaten

¼ cup finely chopped fresh basil

¼ cup finely chopped fresh flat-leaf parsley

¼ teaspoon freshly grated nutmeg

15 (17- by 12-inch) frozen phyllo sheets, thawed

1 stick (½ cup) plus 2 tablespoons unsalted butter, melted

Stir together ricotta, parmesan, egg, and herbs. Add nutmeg and season with salt and pepper.

Put stack of phyllo sheets on a work surface and cover with 2 overlapping sheets of plastic wrap and a damp kitchen towel. Put a sheet of wax paper on work surface and place 1 phyllo sheet on it. Brush phyllo with some melted butter. Top with 2 more phyllo sheets, buttering each.

Preheat oven to 375°F.

Spread ⅓ cup cheese mixture across a short end of phyllo, leaving a 2-inch border on bottom and a 1-inch border on both sides. Fold sides and bottom of phyllo over filling and brush with butter. Using wax paper as a guide, roll up phyllo into a log. Transfer log, seam side down, onto a large buttered baking sheet and brush with some melted butter. Make 4 more logs in same manner, arranging 1½ inches apart on baking sheet. Score top of each log diagonally into 6 pieces, cutting through top layers of phyllo but not into filling. (This will prevent phyllo from crumbling when cut after baking.)

Bake strudels in middle of oven until golden, 30 to 35 minutes. Cool on baking sheet on a rack 15 minutes before slicing. Serve warm or at room temperature.

COOKS' NOTE

• Strudels may be assembled (but not baked) 1 week ahead and frozen, wrapped well in plastic wrap, on a baking sheet. Thaw before baking.

SERVES 10 TO 12

Wild rice salad

1 lb wild rice

¼ cup fresh orange juice

3 tablespoons chopped shallot

3 tablespoons balsamic vinegar

2 teaspoons Dijon mustard

1 teaspoon minced garlic

½ cup extra-virgin olive oil

1 cup long-grain white rice

1½ cups water

2 cups hickory nuts or chopped pecans, toasted

1¼ cups chopped fresh flat-leaf parsley

¾ cup dried apricots, thinly sliced

¾ cup dried cranberries

Rinse wild rice in a sieve under cold water, then combine with cold water to cover by 2 inches in a 5-quart pot. Simmer, covered, until tender, 45 minutes to 1 hour.

MAKE VINAIGRETTE WHILE WILD RICE SIMMERS:

Whisk together juice, shallot, vinegar, mustard, and garlic. Gradually add oil, whisking until emulsified, and season with salt and pepper.

COOK WHITE RICE:

After wild rice has been simmering 20 minutes, boil white rice and 1½ cups water in a 1½-quart heavy saucepan, uncovered and undisturbed, until steam holes appear on surface, about 8 minutes. Reduce heat to very low and cook, covered and undisturbed, 15 minutes more. Remove from heat and let stand, covered, 5 minutes.

ASSEMBLE SALAD:

Rinse cooked wild rice in a sieve under cold water, then drain. Stir together rices, vinaigrette, nuts, parsley, dried fruit, and salt and pepper to taste. Serve at room temperature.

COOKS' NOTE

• Salad keeps, covered and chilled, 3 days.

SERVES 12

Herb-roasted turkey breast

2 large garlic cloves

1 teaspoon dried marjoram

1 teaspoon dried thyme

1 teaspoon dried oregano, crumbled

1 teaspoon salt

¾ teaspoon black pepper

2 tablespoons extra-virgin olive oil

1 (5- to 7-lb) skinless boneless whole turkey breast

¼ cup chicken broth

½ cup mayonnaise

½ cup sour cream or whole-milk yogurt

2 tablespoons finely chopped fresh flat-leaf parsley

½ teaspoon fresh lemon juice, or to taste

Mash garlic, dried herbs, salt, and pepper to a paste with a mortar and pestle or blender, then stir in oil.

Pat turkey dry and rub all over with paste. Transfer to a 13- by 9-inch flameproof glass baking dish. Chill, covered, at least 8 hours. (Bring turkey to room temperature before roasting.)

Preheat oven to 350°F.

Roast in middle of oven, uncovered, until an instant-read thermometer registers 170°F when inserted 2 inches into thickest part of breast, 1 to 1¼ hours. Transfer to a platter and cover loosely with foil. Let stand 20 minutes.

MAKE SAUCE WHILE TURKEY STANDS:
Pour broth into baking dish and deglaze by boiling over high heat, stirring and scraping up brown bits. Transfer to a bowl, then skim off any fat and cool to warm. Add any juices that have accumulated on platter. Whisk in mayonnaise and sour cream until smooth. Stir in parsley and season with lemon juice and salt and pepper.

Slice turkey and serve with sauce.

COOKS' NOTES

• Turkey (rubbed with paste) can chill up to 1 day.

• Turkey and sauce are also good served at room temperature; both can be made 1 day ahead and kept separately, covered and chilled.

SERVES 10 TO 12

Sautéed sugar snap peas

¼ lb shallots, thinly sliced (1 cup)

3 tablespoons olive oil

3 lb sugar snap peas, trimmed

Cook ½ cup shallots in 1½ tablespoons oil in a deep 12-inch skillet over moderately high heat, stirring frequently, until lightly browned, 3 to 4 minutes. Add half of peas and sauté, stirring frequently, until just crisp-tender, about 4 minutes. Transfer to a large bowl. Cook remaining shallots and peas in remaining oil in same manner, then transfer to bowl and season with salt and pepper.

SERVES 10 TO 12

Blossom-topped cupcakes

FOR CUPCAKES

2 cups cake flour (not self-rising)

1 teaspoon baking powder

½ teaspoon salt

2 sticks (1 cup) unsalted butter, softened

1½ cups granulated sugar

4 large eggs

¼ cup whole milk

1 teaspoon vanilla

FOR FROSTING

2 (8-oz) packages cream cheese, softened

1 cup confectioners sugar

1 teaspoon fresh lemon juice

¼ teaspoon rosewater (optional)

Garnish: nontoxic and organic (pesticide-free) small roses and pansies and scented geranium leaves (see box on page 115) and blackberries dusted with confectioners sugar

Special equipment: 16 (2½-inch) paper muffin-cup liners

MAKE CUPCAKES:

Preheat oven to 350°F and line 16 (⅓-cup) muffin cups with muffin-cup liners.

Sift together flour, baking powder, and salt. Beat together butter and granulated sugar in a large bowl with an electric mixer until light and fluffy. Add eggs 1 at a time, beating well after each addition, and, with mixer at low speed, beat in milk and vanilla until just combined (batter will separate). Add flour mixture in 3 batches, beating until just combined after each addition.

Divide batter among muffin cups and bake in middle of oven until a tester comes out clean, about 20 minutes. Cool cupcakes in pan on a rack 5 minutes, then remove from pan.

MAKE FROSTING:

Beat cream cheese with electric mixer until smooth, then add confectioners sugar and beat at low speed until incorporated. Add lemon juice and rosewater and beat until smooth.

Frost cupcakes.

COOKS' NOTES

• Cupcakes can be baked 1 day ahead and kept in an airtight container at room temperature. Frost and garnish just before serving.

• Frosting may be made 2 days ahead and chilled, covered. Beat frosting until smooth before using.

MAKES 16 CUPCAKES

WHEN WE DECIDED to garnish cupcakes with nothing but fresh edible flowers, we were unprepared for just how exquisitely beautiful the little offerings would be! Cupcakes covered with Johnny-jump-ups and roses became Victorian nosegays; those crowned with just one velvety deep-purple pansy took a turn for the dramatic.

You should be aware, however, that not all flowers are fair game. When choosing edible flowers, it is *absolutely essential* that they be unsprayed and organically grown. We ordered ours from Indian Rock Produce, (800) 882-0512 (a box of 50 pansies goes for about $15), and Diamond Organic (800) 922-2396; they are also available from farmers markets, some specialty produce shops, and maybe even your own backyard. Do not eat flowers picked from the roadside or those from garden centers, nurseries, or florists.

After talking with Cathy Wilkinson Barash, a leading expert on the subject, we compiled the following short—and far from complete—list of flowers that are safe to eat or use as garnish, as well as some to steer clear of. If you're at all uncertain about a variety, avoid it. As a general rule, eat only the petals and bear in mind that many nontoxic flowers may be harmful in large amounts. People with hay fever, asthma, or allergies should avoid eating flowers altogether.

Nontoxic: chrysanthemum, day lily, dianthus, geranium, hibiscus, honeysuckle, Johnny-jump-up, lilac, marigold, nasturtium, pansy, rose, violet.

Toxic: anemone, azalea, daffodil, daisy, delphinium, hyacinth, impatiens, lily of the valley, morning glory, oleander, orchid, petunia, sweet pea.

—JANE DANIELS LEAR

Graduation day party

OUR GRADUATION DAY PARTY is ideal for a wide range of guests, including recent college graduates with astonishing appetites, proud grandmothers, and everyone in between. The food is decidedly down-home—crab melts, peanuts, black-eyed peas, peaches, and spicy slaw each make an appearance, with pulled barbecued chicken on corn bread taking center stage. And, of course, orangeade and beer help keep the tone informal. This is such an easygoing menu, you might want to consider it for all sorts of small outdoor gatherings, especially family reunions or the Fourth of July.

Orangeade

TO SERVE 12, YOU MAY WANT TO MAKE AT LEAST 2 BATCHES.

6 cups fresh orange juice

4½ cups chilled seltzer or club soda

Garnish: orange slices

Stir together juice and seltzer in a large pitcher and serve in tall glasses half-filled with ice.

MAKES ABOUT 10½ CUPS

Peanut-mango salsa with jícama chips

½ teaspoon cumin seeds

⅛ teaspoon cayenne

1½ tablespoons olive oil

2 mangoes, peeled and coarsely chopped

3 tablespoons fresh lime juice

1 cup cocktail peanuts, coarsely chopped

1 (1-lb) *jícama*, peeled, quartered, and thinly sliced

Cook cumin seeds and cayenne in oil in a small skillet over low heat until fragrant, about 1 minute, then transfer to a bowl. Stir in mango, lime juice, and peanuts and season with salt and pepper. Transfer half of salsa to a food processor and pulse until finely chopped, then fold back into remaining salsa.

Serve salsa with *jícama* for dipping.

COOKS' NOTE

• Salsa can be made 1 day ahead and chilled, covered.

MAKES ABOUT 2½ CUPS

Crab melts

1 (16- by 4-inch) loaf soft Italian bread, halved horizontally

1 lb jumbo lump crabmeat, picked over and shredded

1 bunch scallions, chopped (1 cup)

½ cup mayonnaise

½ teaspoon fresh lemon juice

¼ teaspoon cayenne

5 oz Swiss cheese, shredded (1⅓ cups)

Preheat oven to 450°F.

Trim crusts from top and bottom of bread halves to make 2 large slices, each about 16 inches long and 1 inch thick. Arrange bread in 1 layer on a large baking sheet.

Stir together crabmeat, scallion, mayonnaise, lemon juice, cayenne, and salt and pepper to taste. Divide mixture between bread slices, spreading evenly, then sprinkle with cheese.

Bake in upper third of oven until cheese melts and crabmeat is heated through, about 15 minutes. Transfer crab melts to a cutting board and cut each diagonally into 8 pieces.

COOKS' NOTE

• Crab mixture can be made 1 day ahead and chilled, covered.

MAKES 16 HORS D'OEUVRES

Another crowd-pleasing option: ham

NOTHING BEATS A HAM. It's easy, reliable, and if you think you might have a few extra guests, it will give you the assurance of having plenty of food.

Fans of **smoky ham** will love the luscious cob-smoked number from Dakin Farm, in Vermont (800-993-2546). Another excellent choice is Nueske's (800-392-2266).

For a **fresh-pork taste,** try Tobin brand, available from Jefferson Market (212-533-3377); the sugar-cured smoked ham from Gwaltney (800-292-2773); or the one from Ham I Am! (800-742-6426).

The Honeybaked Ham Company (800-343-4267) offers **the sweetest ham** around; another with overall **general appeal** can be ordered from Harry and David (800-547-3033). Finally, S. Wallace Edwards and Sons (800-222-4267) sells some of Virginia's very best **country ham**.

Once you've found a ham you like, you may want to add a glaze and/or stud it with cloves. If it's precooked and you wish to reheat it, the rule of thumb is 10 minutes per pound in the middle of a 325°F oven.

Pulled barbecued chicken on corn bread

6½ lb skinless chicken thighs (24)

1 tablespoon paprika

2 teaspoons salt

1 teaspoon black pepper

½ teaspoon cayenne

½ teaspoon ground cumin

1½ cups ketchup

¾ cup unsulfured molasses

¾ cup cider vinegar

2 tablespoons Tabasco, or to taste

Accompaniment: corn bread (recipe follows)

Preheat oven to 350°F.

Pat chicken dry. Stir together paprika, salt, pepper, cayenne, and cumin and rub all over chicken. Arrange thighs in 1 layer in a lightly oiled shallow (1-inch-deep) baking pan and bake in middle of oven until cooked through, about 45 minutes. When chicken is cool enough to handle, pull meat from bones and coarsely shred.

Pour pan juices into a bowl and skim off fat (you will have about 1 cup), then simmer juices with ketchup, molasses, vinegar, and Tabasco in a 4-quart pot over moderate heat, 5 minutes. Stir in shredded chicken and simmer gently 5 minutes.

Serve chicken over split pieces of corn bread.

COOKS' NOTE

• Chicken can made 2 days ahead and cooled completely before being chilled, covered. Reheat before serving.

SERVES 12

Corn bread

3 cups cornmeal (preferably stone ground)

1 cup all-purpose flour

1 tablespoon plus 1 teaspoon baking powder

2 teaspoons baking soda

1½ teaspoons salt

2½ cups well-shaken buttermilk

2 large eggs, lightly beaten

1½ sticks (¾ cup) unsalted butter, cut into pieces

Preheat oven to 400°F.

Mix together cornmeal, flour, baking powder, baking soda, and salt in a large bowl, then whisk in buttermilk and eggs until well blended. Melt butter in a 13- by 9-inch metal baking pan in middle of oven. Carefully stir butter into batter, then pour batter into pan, spreading evenly.

Bake corn bread until lightly browned and firm to the touch, about 20 minutes. Cool on a rack 5 minutes, then cut into 24 pieces.

SERVES 12

Black-eyed pea salad

4 cups water

1 tablespoon kosher salt

2 (1-lb) or 3 (10-oz) packages frozen black-eyed peas

3 celery stalks, cut into ½-inch dice

6 carrots, cut into ½-inch dice

1 bunch scallions, chopped

¼ cup chopped fresh dill

¼ cup fresh lemon juice

6 tablespoons extra-virgin olive oil

Bring water and kosher salt to a boil in a large pot, then cook peas until tender but not mushy, about 20 minutes. Drain well and cool slightly. Toss gently with celery, carrots, scallions, and dill in a large bowl. Whisk together lemon juice and oil in a small bowl and season with salt and pepper. Toss salad with dressing and season with salt and pepper.

COOKS' NOTE
• Salad may be made 2 hours ahead and kept at room temperature.

SERVES 12 (MAKES ABOUT 10 CUPS)

Spicy slaw

1½ cups mayonnaise

½ cup cider vinegar

⅓ cup sugar, or to taste

1 tablespoon Tabasco, or to taste

2 teaspoons kosher salt, or to taste

½ teaspoon black pepper, or to taste

4 lb mixed cabbages such as green, red, and Savoy, thinly sliced

3 cups cherry tomatoes, halved

1 large sweet onion, thinly sliced

3 cucumbers, peeled, seeded, and diced

1 small red bell pepper, cut into thin strips

1 small yellow bell pepper, cut into thin strips

Whisk together mayonnaise, vinegar, sugar, Tabasco, salt, and pepper until sugar is dissolved, then toss with vegetables.

COOKS' NOTE
• Slaw may be made 1 day ahead and chilled, covered.

SERVES 12

IF YOU LIKE YOUR SLAW WITH A BIT OF A KICK, YOU'LL LOVE THIS ONE FROM LOUIS OSTEEN.

Frozen lime pies

3⅓ sticks (1⅔ cups) unsalted butter

2 cups finely ground graham crackers

1½ cups granulated sugar

6 large limes

5 large eggs

2 cups heavy cream

⅓ cup confectioners sugar

MAKE CRUST:

Preheat oven to 375°F.

Melt 1⅓ sticks butter, then pulse with graham cracker crumbs and ½ cup granulated sugar in a food processor until crumbs are evenly moistened. Divide mixture between 2 (9-inch) pie plates, pressing firmly over bottom and up sides with fingers. Bake crusts 1 at a time in middle of oven until lightly browned, 6 to 8 minutes, and transfer to racks to cool.

MAKE FILLING:

Finely grate enough zest from limes to measure 2 teaspoons, then squeeze enough juice to measure 1 cup. Whisk together zest, juice, remaining cup granulated sugar, and eggs in a metal bowl. Cut remaining 2 sticks butter into tablespoons and add to bowl. Set bowl over a saucepan of simmering water and cook mixture, whisking constantly, until thickened and smooth and an instant-read thermometer registers 160°F, about 5 minutes. Pour curd through a very fine sieve into a bowl and chill, its surface covered with wax paper (to prevent a skin forming), until cold, about 2 hours. (Alternatively, quickly chill curd by placing bowl in a larger bowl of ice water and stirring occasionally until cold.)

Beat cream with confectioners sugar until it just holds soft peaks, then fold into curd. Divide filling between pie crusts and freeze pies until firm, at least 2 hours. (If making ahead, let pies freeze 2 hours before wrapping in plastic wrap.) Let stand at room temperature 30 minutes before cutting and serving.

COOKS' NOTE

• Pies can be frozen up to 1 week ahead, wrapped well in plastic wrap.

MAKES 2 (9-INCH) PIES

Peaches with raspberry syrup

2 (10-oz) packages frozen raspberries in syrup, thawed

½ cup plus 1 tablespoon peach schnapps

¼ cup fresh lemon juice

5 lb ripe peaches, peeled and cut into ½-inch wedges

2 tablespoons sugar, or to taste

Purée raspberries with syrup in a blender, then force through a very fine sieve into a bowl. Stir in 1 tablespoon peach schnapps and 1 teaspoon lemon juice, then chill, covered.

Toss peaches with remaining ½ cup schnapps, sugar, and remaining lemon juice. Chill, covered, until cold, about 1 hour.

Serve peaches drizzled with raspberry syrup.

COOKS' NOTE

• Peaches and sauce can be prepared 1 day ahead and kept separately, covered and chilled.

SERVES 12

Pool party for the kids

IT'S THE LAST DAY OF SCHOOL before summer vacation and your house (or rather, your pool) has been designated party central. Now you just need to make sure you have enough inflatable tubes and appropriate kid-friendly foods. To keep it simple (without picking up the phone and ordering in), why not make pizzas with English muffins and add a few easy, tasty treats. We guarantee that none of these recipes will wear the hostess out. (The kids will manage that.)

Honey-soy chicken wings

⅔ cup honey

⅔ cup soy sauce (preferably tamari)

2 tablespoons cider vinegar

3½ lb chicken wings, tips discarded and wings halved through joints

Stir together honey, soy sauce, and cider vinegar. Measure out ¼ cup marinade and reserve. Toss wings with remaining marinade and transfer to a heavy-duty sealable plastic bag. Marinate, turning bag occasionally, at least 8 hours.

Preheat oven to 375°F.

Discard marinade and arrange wings in 1 layer in a large shallow baking pan. Roast in middle of oven 15 minutes, then turn wings over and roast 12 minutes more.

Preheat broiler.

Baste wings with half of reserved marinade and broil 4 to 6 inches from heat 2 minutes. Turn wings over and baste with remaining marinade, then broil 2 minutes more. Serve wings warm, room temperature, or cold.

SERVES 10

Miniature tomato and mozzarella pizzas

1 medium onion, chopped

2 tablespoons plus 2 teaspoons extra-virgin olive oil

1 teaspoon unsalted butter

1 small garlic clove, minced

1 (14-oz) can crushed tomatoes

¼ teaspoon sugar

¼ teaspoon dried oregano, crumbled

Pinch of dried thyme

5 sandwich-size English muffins, split

1 lb fresh mozzarella, coarsely grated

Cook onion in 2 teaspoons oil and butter in a saucepan over moderate heat, stirring occasionally, until softened, 4 to 5 minutes. Add garlic and cook, stirring, 1 minute. Add tomatoes, sugar, and herbs and simmer, stirring frequently, until thickened, about 20 minutes. Season with salt and pepper.

Preheat broiler.

Arrange 5 muffin halves in 1 layer on a broiler pan and lightly brush both sides with some of remaining 2 tablespoons oil. Broil, turning once, until toasted, 2 to 4 minutes total (watch carefully to avoid burning). Transfer toasts, cut sides up, to a large baking sheet. Toast remaining muffin halves in same manner.

Preheat oven to 450°F.

Spread 2 tablespoons sauce on each muffin and sprinkle each with cheese. Bake until hot and cheese is bubbling, about 15 minutes. Cool on racks 5 minutes before serving.

SERVES 10

Crunchy noodle salad with orange-sesame dressing

2 (3-oz) packages ramen noodles (discard seasoning packets)

1¾ oz sliced or slivered almonds (½ cup)

2 tablespoons sesame seeds

1 tablespoon vegetable oil

¼ cup fresh orange juice

¼ cup cider vinegar

2 tablespoons sugar

2 tablespoons soy sauce (preferably *tamari*)

1 teaspoon toasted sesame oil

½ small head green cabbage, finely shredded (4 cups)

2 carrots, shredded

4 scallions, chopped

Preheat oven to 350°F.

Crumble noodles into a large shallow (1-inch-deep) baking pan, then toss with almonds, sesame seeds, and vegetable oil. Bake in middle of oven, stirring occasionally, until golden, about 15 minutes. Cool in pan on a rack.

Whisk together orange juice, vinegar, sugar, soy sauce, and sesame oil in a large bowl until sugar is dissolved. Just before serving, add noodle mixture, cabbage, carrots, and scallions and toss to combine. Season with salt and pepper.

COOKS' NOTES

• Noodles may be baked 4 hours ahead and kept at room temperature in an airtight container.

• Dressing may be prepared 4 hours ahead and chilled, covered. Toss with noodle mixture and vegetables just before serving.

SERVES 10

Strawberry ice-cream frappés

8 cups milk

1 qt strawberry ice cream, softened

6 cups frozen strawberries (from three 20-oz packages)

Garnish: whole fresh strawberries

Blend 2 cups milk, 1 cup ice cream, and 1½ cups frozen berries in blender until frothy. Pour into tall glasses. Repeat 3 more times with remaining ingredients in same manner.

MAKES 10 (1½-CUP) DRINKS

Giant chocolate cookies

FOR EXTRA CHOCOLATEY COOKIES, STIR A 12-OZ PACKAGE OF CHOCOLATE CHIPS INTO THE DOUGH.

1¾ cups all-purpose flour

¾ cup unsweetened cocoa powder (preferably Dutch-process)

1 teaspoon baking soda

1 teaspoon salt

½ teaspoon cinnamon

2 sticks (1 cup) unsalted butter, softened

1½ cups sugar

1 teaspoon vanilla

2 large eggs

Preheat oven to 375°F.

Sift together flour, cocoa powder, baking soda, salt, and cinnamon. Beat together butter, sugar, and vanilla until pale and fluffy. Add eggs 1 at a time, beating well after each addition, then stir in flour mixture.

Drop a scant ¼ cup dough for each cookie onto a large greased baking sheet, spacing about 2 inches apart.

Bake cookies in batches in middle of oven, rotating sheet halfway during baking, until cookies are set and dry to touch, 14 to 18 minutes total. Cool on sheet on a rack 3 minutes, then transfer to racks to cool.

COOKS' NOTES:

• A 1½-oz ice cream scoop is a great tool for measuring the dough for each cookie.

• Cookies keep 5 days in an airtight container.

MAKES ABOUT 16 (4-INCH) COOKIES

How to pick a good watermelon

DOES THUMPING the outside really tell you anything? Ed Kee, a cooperative extension specialist at the University of Delaware, says that yes, thumping a whole watermelon detects ripeness (listen for a hollow, resonant sound), but that there is a better gauge. Look at the color of the rind where the melon was resting on the ground. If it's creamy white, that melon is not ripe. Go for rind with yellowish-orange "ground color." If you're buying cut sections, pick the reddest flesh. It's not a foolproof indicator, as the deeper color can be the result of several factors, but it can reflect maturity and, therefore, a higher sugar content. And that annoying mealy texture? It's caused by too much fertilizer, too much rain near harvest, or too much time at market. Once picked, watermelons with seeds continue to ripen and deepen in color; the seeds trigger maturation. Seedless varieties are different; once picked, the ripening stops.

—KEMP MINIFIE

Milestone birthday

BIRTHDAYS ARE ALWAYS SPECIAL,

but the big ones (i.e., the ones that end in

zeroes) deserve extra recognition. Our

Mediterranean-inspired menu and glorious

four-layer birthday cake should do the trick.

Although the cake may look daunting, it's

actually much easier to master than you

think. A pastry bag, a few basic decorating

tips, and the information on pages 134–135

are all you'll need. You can simply omit the

frills, of course, if it all seems a bit over-the-

top. But since you're probably only going to

do this once every ten years, why not pull

out all the stops?

Grilled scallops with tomato-onion relish

½ cup finely chopped red onion

¾ teaspoon salt

1 large tomato, seeded and chopped

4 teaspoons red-wine vinegar

1 teaspoon sugar

2 tablespoons chopped fresh dill

24 sea scallops (1½ lb), tough muscles removed from sides if necessary

Vegetable oil for brushing grill

Prepare grill for cooking.

Soak onion in 1 cup water with ½ teaspoon salt 15 minutes, then drain. Stir together onion, tomato, vinegar, sugar, and remaining ¼ teaspoon salt and let stand 20 minutes. Drain relish in a sieve, discarding liquid, then stir in dill.

COOK SCALLOPS WHILE RELISH STANDS:
Pat scallops dry and season with salt and pepper. Grill scallops in 2 batches on lightly oiled grill rack, turning once, until just cooked through, 4 to 5 minutes.

Arrange scallops on a platter and top each with a teaspoon of relish.

COOKS' NOTE:
• Alternatively, you can grill scallops in a well-seasoned ridged grill pan over high heat.

MAKES **24** HORS D'OEUVRES

Feta with pepper honey

1 lb feta

2½ teaspoons black peppercorns, coarsely cracked

⅓ cup honey

Accompaniment: crackers

Pat feta dry and put on a platter. Stir together pepper and honey in a measuring cup and pour over feta.

SERVES **8** GENEROUSLY

THINLY SLICED, THIS FETA ALSO MAKES A LOVELY DESSERT.

Green olive, lemon, and garlic–roasted leg of lamb with potatoes and pan gravy

1 large lemon

½ cup brine-cured green olives (preferably Italian), pitted

6 large garlic cloves

⅓ cup packed fresh flat-leaf parsley

6 tablespoons olive oil

4 lb boiling potatoes (preferably Yukon Gold), peeled and cut into 1½-inch pieces

1 (7-lb) leg of lamb, pelvic bone removed and lamb tied

½ tablespoon all-purpose flour

½ tablespoon unsalted butter

½ cup dry white wine

½ cup water

Garnish: lemon halves and olive branches

PREPARE LAMB:

Preheat oven to 450° F.

Remove zest from lemon with a vegetable peeler and reserve lemon. Finely chop zest, olives, garlic, and parsley with 3 tablespoons oil in a food processor.

Toss potatoes with remaining 3 tablespoons oil to coat in a large flameproof roasting pan and season with salt and pepper. Arrange lamb on potatoes and cut small slits all over lamb with tip of a sharp small knife. Rub olive mixture over lamb, pushing it into slits. Halve reserved lemon and squeeze juice over lamb. Season lamb with salt and pepper and roast with potatoes in middle of oven 20 minutes.

Reduce temperature to 350°F.

Roast lamb and potatoes, loosening potatoes from pan with a metal spatula and turning them occasionally, 1 hour more, or until a meat thermometer inserted into thickest part of meat (do not touch bone) registers 135°F. Transfer lamb to a cutting board and let stand while making gravy. Transfer potatoes to a large bowl and keep warm, covered.

MAKE GRAVY:

Blend together flour and butter in a cup with your fingers. Add wine and water to roasting pan and deglaze by boiling over moderately high heat, stirring and scraping up brown bits. Transfer to a small saucepan and bring to a boil. Whisk in flour mixture, whisking until incorporated, and simmer gravy, stirring occasionally, 1 minute. Remove any potato pieces from gravy with a slotted spoon.

Serve lamb with gravy and potatoes.

SERVES **8** GENEROUSLY

Fennel and romaine salad with marinated roasted peppers

3 large red bell peppers, seeded and quartered lengthwise

2 tablespoons balsamic vinegar

1 tablespoon packed light brown sugar

¼ cup extra-virgin olive oil

1 large fennel bulb (sometimes called anise), stalks trimmed flush with bulb and discarded

1 large head romaine, torn into bite-size pieces

Special equipment: a *mandoline* or other manual slicer

Preheat broiler.

Broil bell peppers, skin sides up, in batches on a broiler pan 4 to 6 inches from heat until skins are blistered and lightly blackened, 4 to 6 minutes. Transfer to a large bowl and cool, covered. Remove and discard skins from peppers and cut flesh into 1- by ¼-inch pieces.

Whisk together vinegar and sugar in a large bowl until sugar dissolves, then whisk in oil. Toss red peppers with dressing and season with salt and pepper. Marinate, covered and chilled, at least 8 hours. Let peppers come to room temperature before serving.

Trim any tough outer layers from fennel bulb, then quarter bulb and thinly slice lengthwise with *mandoline*. Cut slices lengthwise into ¼-inch strips.

Toss together fennel, romaine, and peppers and season with salt and pepper.

COOKS' NOTE
• Romaine and fennel can be prepared 1 day ahead and kept separately in sealable plastic bags, chilled.

SERVES **8**

Asparagus with parmesan

3 lb asparagus, trimmed, and peeled if desired

2 tablespoons extra-virgin olive oil

⅔ cup freshly grated parmesan (2 oz)

Cook asparagus in a large pot of boiling salted water until just crisp-tender, 3 to 4 minutes, then transfer with tongs to paper towels to drain.

Preheat oven to 425°F.

Arrange half of asparagus in 1 layer in an oiled 13- by 9-inch baking dish. Drizzle with 1 tablespoon olive oil. Season with salt and pepper and sprinkle with ⅓ cup cheese. Repeat layering with remaining asparagus, oil, and cheese in same manner.

Bake, covered, in middle of oven 10 minutes, then uncover and bake until hot and cheese is bubbling, about 10 minutes more.

SERVES **8**

Golden cake with chocolate sour cream frosting

3½ cups cake flour (not self-rising)

1 tablespoon baking powder

¾ teaspoon baking soda

1 teaspoon salt

2 sticks (1 cup) unsalted butter, softened

2 cups sugar

4 large eggs at room temperature

2 teaspoons vanilla

2 cups sour cream

Chocolate sour cream frosting
(page 132)

Garnish: brown sugar buttercream
(page 132)

Preheat oven to 350°F. Butter 2 (9- by 2-inch) round cake pans and line bottoms of each with rounds of wax or parchment paper. Butter paper and dust pans with flour, knocking out excess.

Sift together flour, baking powder, baking soda, and salt. Beat together butter and sugar in a large bowl with an electric mixer until light and fluffy. Add eggs 1 at a time, beating well after each addition, then beat in vanilla. Add half of flour mixture and mix at low speed until just blended. Add sour cream, mixing until just combined, then add remaining flour mixture, mixing at low speed until batter is smooth.

Divide batter between pans, smoothing tops. Bake in middle of oven until cake is springy to the touch and a tester comes out clean, 30 to 40 minutes. Cool in pans on racks 10 minutes. Invert onto racks, remove paper, and cool completely.

Trim tops of cooled cake layers if necessary with a long serrated knife to make flat and level. Halve each layer horizontally with serrated knife to make a total of 4 layers (see box on page 134). Put 1 cake layer on a cake plate and spread with ¾ cup frosting, then layer remaining cake layers using ¾ cup frosting between each layer. Frost top and sides of cake with remaining frosting.

COOKS' NOTES

• Cake layers can be made 1 day ahead of assembling and kept, wrapped well in plastic wrap, at room temperature.

• Cake can be assembled 1 day ahead and chilled in a cake keeper or loosely covered with plastic wrap (use toothpicks to hold wrap away from frosting). Bring to room temperature before serving.

• This batter can be baked in a 13- by 9- by 2-inch pan 50 to 55 minutes; or in 30 (½-cup) muffin cups about 25 minutes.

• We used 2 pastry bags, one fitted with an ⅛-inch plain tip and the other fitted with a ¾-inch ribbon (basketweave) tip, and couplers to decorate our cake, but it won't be any less attractive or delicious if you decide simply to use candles. (For more on cake decorating, see box on pages 134–135.)

SERVES 12

Chocolate sour cream frosting

1¼ lb fine-quality milk chocolate, finely chopped

10 oz fine-quality semisweet chocolate, finely chopped

3 cups sour cream

2 teaspoons vanilla

Melt chocolates in a double boiler or a large metal bowl set over a saucepan of simmering water, stirring occasionally. Remove bowl from heat, then whisk in sour cream and vanilla. Cool to room temperature, stirring occasionally (frosting will become thick enough to spread). You must work quickly and spread the frosting before it becomes too thick. (If icing does become stiff, reheat over simmering water, then cool and try again.)

MAKES ABOUT 4 CUPS

Brown sugar buttercream

3 large egg whites at room temperature

⅛ teaspoon salt

1 cup packed dark brown sugar

½ cup water

½ teaspoon fresh lemon juice

3 sticks (1½ cups) unsalted butter, cut into pieces and softened

2 teaspoons vanilla

Special equipment: a candy thermometer

Combine egg whites and salt in a large bowl. Stir together brown sugar and water in a small heavy saucepan and bring to a boil over moderately high heat, washing down side of pan with a pastry brush dipped in water. When sugar syrup reaches boil, start beating whites with an electric mixer at medium-high speed until frothy, then add lemon juice and beat at medium speed until whites just hold soft peaks. (Do not beat again until sugar syrup is ready.)

Meanwhile, put candy thermometer into sugar syrup and continue boiling until syrup reaches 238–242°F. Immediately remove from heat and pour into a heatproof 1-cup glass measure. Slowly pour hot syrup in a thin stream down side of bowl into egg whites, beating constantly at high speed. Beat meringue, scraping down bowl with a rubber spatula, until meringue is cool to the touch, about 6 minutes. (It's important that meringue is properly cooled before proceeding.)

Gradually add butter 1 piece at a time with mixer at medium speed, beating well after each addition until incorporated. (If meringue is too warm and buttercream looks soupy after some of butter is added, briefly chill bottom of bowl in a large bowl filled with ice water for a few seconds before continuing to beat in remaining butter.) Continue beating until buttercream is smooth. (Mixture may look curdled before all of butter is added, but will come back together before beating is finished.) Add vanilla and beat 1 minute.

COOKS' NOTE:

• Buttercream can be made 1 week ahead and chilled, covered, or frozen 1 month. Bring to room temperature (do not use a microwave) and beat with electric mixer before using.

MAKES ABOUT 3½ CUPS

Decorating is a piece of cake

A BIRTHDAY CAKE, by its very nature, requires some sort of embellishment. Yet it's important to keep a very valuable lesson in mind: Don't go overboard.

Before a dollop of frosting makes contact with your cake, be sure to have all the necessary tools clean and close at hand. (Most are available at cookware shops and by mail order from New York Cake & Baking Distributors, 800-942-2539.) A long narrow flat metal spatula, particularly the offset kind, is extremely helpful for spreading wide swaths of frosting. If you plan to create a piped design like the one shown on page 133, you'll need two good-sized pastry bags (one for each color of frosting), the proper tips, and the couplers to attach them to the bags (they provide an extra measure of security). A cake-decorating turntable, which is similar to a lazy Susan, isn't essential but certainly makes you feel like a pro, and it does make smoothing the frosting on large cakes a breeze. (If you do use a turntable, then you'll also want a cardboard round to rest the cake on and two rigid pancake turner-style spatulas to move it from turntable to cake plate.)

We try to avoid splitting cake layers, but it makes sense for a big four-layer cake like the one here (more layers mean a better ratio of frosting to cake). We like to insert long wooden skewers horizontally into the cake halfway up the side in about eight places around the outside. Then, resting an 11- to 12-inch knife (preferably serrated) against the sticks, we use a long sawing motion to cut the cake layer in two (see photo above).

Prepping your cake for frosting is a lot like prepping a wall for painting. Cake crumbs, like dust and grime, are the enemy. Once your layers are stacked and lightly brushed free of loose crumbs, apply what's called a crumb coat (think primer), a thin layer of frosting all around the top and side that seals the remaining crumbs in place. Chill the cake to firm up the frosting, then watch as the second coat goes on effortlessly.

Sara Neumeier, a freelance food stylist, taught us a thing or two when she styled our birthday cake. One of her tricks will be a boon to anyone with a bad back: Before she piped the variegated lines on the cake, she moved the cake on its pedestal plate from the kitchen counter to a table, then propped up the base of the plate with a folded towel so that the cake tilted away from her (see photo below). Pulling up a chair, she was then in a comfortable, eye-level position for steady-armed work with a pastry bag and the cake didn't budge—when Neumeier assembled it, she glued the first layer to the plate with frosting.

In order to pipe the frosting in straight lines, Neumeier marked the cake first by gently pressing a wooden skewer lengthwise at intervals around the smoothly frosted side (see photo, right). Then she piped frosting over the

marks. (Note that the pastry bag action is from bottom to top, not the reverse.) She only made indications for the wide, corrugated bands; the skinnier lines are meant to be free-form.

The best way to protect your masterpiece is to keep it in a cake keeper. It may seem old-fashioned, but there's no better way to preserve the decoration on the outside and the moisture on the inside. We love the elegance of a glass dome if your cake is staying put, but if it has to travel, invest in a plastic version, preferably with handles.

—KEMP MINIFIE

THE HOT WEATHER

has arrived, and it's time to
fire up the grill. Here we've
dreamed up five inspired
cookouts—for steak, pork,
chicken, and seafood—that
sparkle with the best produce
that the summer has to offer.
But don't delay. One minute
the tomatoes are plump, the
peaches are firm, and then
before you know it, they're
gone. You won't want to miss
the chance to entertain so
effortlessly, so wonderfully.

Steak on the grill

STEAK AND POTATO SALAD might sound conventional, but there are a few chef's secrets here worth paying attention to—like coating the meat with a simple spice rub for extraordinary flavor and dressing potato salads healthfully with fresh herbs, a splash of olive oil, and a bit of balsamic vinegar or lemon juice (absolutely no mayonnaise). There are green beans, too, with a sensational mustard-seed vinaigrette that you'll want to try on other vegetables time and time again. The scrumptious blackberry pie is summer itself!

Red pepper and arugula spirals

8 oz cream cheese, softened

1 small garlic clove, minced

½ teaspoon salt

¼ to ½ teaspoon cracked black pepper

2 tablespoons chopped fresh flat-leaf parsley

1 teaspoon chopped fresh thyme

8 (7-inch) flour tortillas

3 (7-oz) jars roasted red peppers, drained, patted dry, and chopped

1 bunch arugula

Stir together cream cheese, garlic, salt, pepper, parsley, and thyme.

Spread 2 tablespoons cream cheese mixture evenly on each tortilla. Top each with 2 tablespoons roasted peppers and 3 arugula leaves, leaving a ¼-inch border around edge. Tightly roll up tortillas and wrap each tightly in plastic wrap. Chill 30 minutes.

Discard plastic wrap and trim ½ inch from ends of each roll. Cut each into 4 pieces and serve, cut sides up, on a plate.

MAKES 32 HORS D'OEUVRES

Grilled spiced rib-eye steaks

8 (1-inch-thick) bone-in rib-eye steaks (each 1 lb)

¼ teaspoon ground allspice

1 teaspoon ground cumin

2 tablespoons kosher salt

Prepare grill for cooking.

Let steaks stand at room temperature 30 minutes. Stir together allspice, cumin, and salt. Pat steaks dry and sprinkle spice mixture onto both sides of steaks, pressing to adhere.

Grill steaks in 2 batches on an oiled rack set 5 to 6 inches over glowing coals 4 to 5 minutes on each side, or until an instant-read thermometer inserted horizontally 2 inches into thickest part of meat registers 130°F for medium-rare. Transfer steaks to a platter and let stand 10 minutes.

SERVES 8

Grilled sweet-potato salad

3½ lb sweet potatoes

⅓ cup olive oil

1½ teaspoons salt

1½ teaspoons ground cumin

2 scallions, thinly sliced diagonally

1 tablespoon fresh lime juice

⅓ cup fresh cilantro leaves

Accompaniment: lime wedges

Cover potatoes with salted cold water by 1 inch in a large saucepan and simmer, covered, until just tender, 15 to 30 minutes, depending on size of potatoes. Drain in a colander and rinse under cold water to cool. Peel potatoes with a sharp knife and cut crosswise into ½-inch-thick slices.

While potatoes boil, prepare grill for cooking.

Whisk together oil, salt, and cumin and brush some onto both sides of potato slices, reserving remaining oil.

Grill slices on an oiled rack set 5 to 6 inches over glowing coals until golden brown, about 1 minute on each side, and transfer with tongs to a platter. Sprinkle scallions over potatoes. Whisk lime juice into remaining cumin oil with salt and pepper to taste and drizzle over potatoes. Sprinkle potato salad with cilantro.

COOKS' NOTE

• Toasted pecans or cooked sausage may be added to the salad. Chopped *chipotle* chile in *adobo* sauce makes a nice addition to the dressing.

SERVES 8

Roasted potato, garlic, and red pepper salad

7 garlic cloves, unpeeled

4 lb small boiling potatoes (white, red, or fingerling), halved

2 large red bell peppers, cut into ½-inch pieces

5 tablespoons extra-virgin olive oil

¼ cup balsamic vinegar

½ cup small fresh basil leaves

Preheat oven to 450°F.

Wrap garlic cloves together in foil. Toss potatoes, bell peppers, and 4 tablespoons oil with salt and pepper to taste in a large bowl, then arrange in 1 layer in 2 large shallow baking pans. Roast vegetables in middle and lower thirds of oven (roast garlic simultaneously on either rack), stirring occasionally and switching position of pans halfway through roasting, until potatoes are tender and golden brown, about 35 minutes.

Toss vegetables immediately with 3 tablespoons vinegar in a bowl and cool. Remove garlic from foil and squeeze pulp into a small bowl. Mash garlic with remaining 1 tablespoon oil and 1 tablespoon vinegar with a fork and toss together with vegetables and salt and pepper to taste.

Just before serving, add basil. Serve potato salad at room temperature.

COOKS' NOTE

• Olives, pine nuts, goat cheese, grilled chicken, tuna, or prosciutto may be added to the salad.

SERVES 8

Green beans with red onion and mustard seed vinaigrette

3 tablespoons olive oil

2 tablespoons mustard seeds

⅓ cup red-wine vinegar

1 tablespoon sugar

1 medium red onion, thinly sliced

1½ lb green beans, trimmed

Heat 1 tablespoon oil in a heavy skillet over moderate heat until hot but not smoking, then cook mustard seeds, stirring, until they pop and are 1 shade darker, about 2 minutes. Transfer oil and seeds to a large bowl.

Simmer red-wine vinegar and sugar in a small saucepan, stirring until sugar dissolves, then cool 5 minutes.

Heat remaining 2 tablespoons oil in cleaned skillet over moderately high heat until hot but not smoking, then cook onion, stirring, until golden brown, 8 to 10 minutes. Remove from heat and stir in vinegar mixture, then add to mustard seeds in large bowl.

Have ready a large bowl of ice and cold water. Cook beans in a large pot of boiling salted water until crisp-tender, about 5 minutes. Drain in a colander and plunge into ice water to stop cooking, then drain well. Toss beans with vinaigrette and salt and pepper to taste. Serve at room temperature or chilled.

SERVES **8**

Lattice-top blackberry pie

6 cups blackberries (1¾ lb)

1 to 1¼ cups granulated sugar

¼ cup cornstarch

2 tablespoons unsalted butter, melted

2 tablespoons fresh lemon juice

2 tablespoons water

1 tablespoon quick-cooking tapioca

Pastry dough (recipe follows)

1 egg white, lightly beaten

1 tablespoon sanding (coarse) or granulated sugar

Accompaniment: vanilla ice cream and/or lightly sweetened whipped cream

Place a baking sheet in lower third of oven and preheat to 400°F.

Toss together berries, granulated sugar to taste, cornstarch, butter, lemon juice, water, and tapioca. Let stand, tossing occasionally, 20 minutes.

Roll out 1 piece of dough into a 14-inch round and fit into a 9-inch (4-cup) pie plate. Trim edge, leaving a ½-inch overhang. Chill shell while rolling out top.

Roll out remaining piece of dough into a rough 16- by 11-inch rectangle. Cut crosswise into 11 (1¼-inch-wide) strips with a fluted pastry wheel or a knife.

Stir berry mixture, then spoon evenly into shell. Arrange strips in a tight lattice pattern on top of filling and trim strips close to edge of plate. Roll up and crimp edge. Brush top and edge with egg white and sprinkle all over with sanding sugar.

Bake on hot baking sheet until crust is golden brown and filling is bubbling, 1 hour to 1 hour and 10 minutes. (Check pie after 45 minutes: If edge of crust is browning too quickly, cover edge with foil or a pie crust shield.) Cool completely on a rack.

COOKS' NOTE

• Keep in mind that berries vary in sweetness, so you'll need to adjust the amount of sugar added accordingly.

SERVES **8**

Pastry dough

2½ cups all-purpose flour

1½ sticks (¾ cup) cold unsalted butter, cut into ½-inch cubes

¼ cup cold vegetable shortening

½ teaspoon salt

4 to 6 tablespoons ice water

Blend together flour, butter, shortening, and salt in a bowl with your fingertips or a pastry blender (or pulse in a food processor) until most of mixture resembles coarse meal with rest in small (roughly pea-size) lumps. Drizzle evenly with 4 tablespoons ice water and gently stir with a fork (or pulse in processor) until incorporated. Gently squeeze a small handful: It should hold together without crumbling apart. If it doesn't, add more water, 1 tablespoon at a time, stirring (or pulsing) after each addition until incorporated, continuing to test. (Do not overwork dough or it will become tough.)

Turn dough out onto a work surface and divide into 2 portions. With heel of your hand, smear each portion once in a forward motion to help distribute fat. Gather each portion of dough and form it, rotating on a work surface, into a disk. Wrap disks separately in wax paper and chill until firm, at least 1 hour.

COOKS' NOTE

• Dough can be chilled, wrapped in plastic wrap, up to 1 day.

MAKES ENOUGH FOR A DOUBLE-CRUST 9-INCH PIE

Lobster on the grill

FOR MOST OF US, fresh lobster is the essence of summer. So why not treat your guests to a lobster grill filled with Asian flavors? As you'll see, cooking lobsters is not as tricky (or scary) as you might think (see the box on page 148). Our lobsters are quickly parboiled, then the claws are grilled separately before the tails are basted and grilled. It's as simple as that. The basting sauce—a spicy southeast Asian concoction with cilantro and mint—is also the dipping sauce. Try it with shrimp, too.

Mirin-marinated cherry tomatoes

⅓ cup mirin (Japanese sweet rice wine)

2 tablespoons soy sauce

2 tablespoons seasoned rice vinegar

1 lb cherry tomatoes

1½ tablespoons kosher salt

1 tablespoon black pepper

Stir together mirin, soy sauce, and vinegar.

Have ready a bowl of ice and cold water. Cut a small "×" in stem end of each tomato, then blanch tomatoes in boiling salted water until skins begin to peel away, about 1 minute. Drain in a colander and immediately plunge into ice water to stop cooking. Drain again, then peel tomatoes and discard skins. Toss tomatoes with soy mixture and chill, covered, 8 hours.

Drain tomatoes and transfer to a bowl. Combine salt and pepper on a small plate and serve with tomatoes for dipping.

SERVES 6

Asian noodle salad

¼ cup soy sauce

2 tablespoons seasoned rice vinegar

1 tablespoon Asian sesame oil

½ teaspoon dried hot red pepper flakes

1 garlic clove, minced

2 teaspoons grated peeled fresh ginger

¾ lb thin linguine

1 cup coarsely grated carrot

3 scallions, cut crosswise into thirds and thinly sliced lengthwise

2 tablespoons sesame seeds, toasted

6 radishes, halved and thinly sliced

Stir together soy sauce, vinegar, oil, red pepper flakes, garlic, and ginger.

Cook linguine in a large pot of boiling salted water until just tender, then drain in a colander and rinse under cold water until cool. Toss with dressing, carrot, scallions, sesame seeds, and radishes in a large bowl.

COOKS' NOTE

• Asian noodle salad (before adding sesame seeds and radishes) may be made 4 hours ahead and chilled, covered.

SERVES 6

Grilled lobsters with southeast asian dipping sauce

6 (1¼-lb) live lobsters

3 garlic cloves, minced

⅓ cup Asian fish sauce

⅓ cup fresh lime juice

⅓ cup packed brown sugar

3 tablespoons water

1½ teaspoons Asian chili paste

¼ cup packed fresh cilantro, chopped

¼ cup packed fresh mint, chopped

Garnish: lime halves

Bring an 8-quart kettle three fourths full with water to a boil for lobsters.

Stir together garlic, fish sauce, lime juice, brown sugar, water, and chili paste in a bowl.

Plunge 2 lobsters headfirst into boiling water and cook 3 minutes (lobsters will be only partially cooked). Transfer with tongs to a colander to drain and cool. Return water to a boil and cook remaining 4 lobsters in same manner.

When lobsters are cool enough to handle, twist off tails and break off claws at body of each lobster, discarding bodies. Halve tails (including shells) lengthwise with kitchen shears. (Do not remove tail or claw meat from shells.)

Prepare grill for cooking.

Stir cilantro and mint into dipping sauce. Measure out ¼ cup dipping sauce to use for basting lobster tails. Grill claws on a rack set 5 to 6 inches over glowing coals, covered, turning them occasionally, until liquid bubbles at open ends, about 5 minutes, then transfer to a platter.

Arrange tails on grill, cut sides up, and brush with basting sauce. Grill tails, covered, basting occasionally, 6 minutes, or until meat is opaque.

Serve lobsters with dipping sauce.

COOKS' NOTES

- Asian dipping sauce (before adding cilantro and mint) may be made 1 day ahead and chilled, covered.

- Lobsters may be boiled and sectioned 1 day ahead and chilled, covered. (If making ahead, chill lobster immediately and keep chilled until ready to grill.)

- To satisfy any die-hard lobster-and-butter traditionalists, you might want to serve clarified butter along with the dipping sauce.

SERVES 6

SWEET, BRINY, intensely oceanic, lobster is a great American treasure. The very best place to buy it, of course, is straight off a lobsterman's boat. We can't all be so lucky. The North Atlantic coast is dotted with hundreds of lobster companies that sell primarily to seafood markets and restaurants; many of them have a retail market, many also ship, and many conveniently sell lobsters ready-boiled. If you are buying from a regular fish market, make sure that it's a busy one, with a brisk turnover, and that the lobsters are kept in aerated saltwater tanks, not on shoals of ice. Buy the most energetic ones you can find, and remember that they are strong and fierce, so handle with care. If you can't ferry them straight to the stovetop, refrigerate them as soon as possible. They will keep, wrapped in damp, not wet, newspaper (don't let it dry out) for a day or so. If they start looking feeble, drop everything and cook them pronto. The most common way to cook lobsters is to plunge them headfirst into a large, tall pot of boiling water. Generously salt the water, to preserve the natural brininess of the seafood, and use enough of it or the lobsters will bring down the water temperature, making it tough to gauge the cooking time. Oh, and keep time from the moment you put the lobsters into the pot, not from when the water resumes a rolling boil.

Lobsters, like other crustaceans, outgrow their shells as they mature. They are called "shedders" or "new shells" during the molting period and while they harden their paper-thin large shell. The meat isn't quite as firm as it could be (although it is usually very sweet and tender), and because the lobsters haven't had time to grow into their shells, water collects inside the carapace. (If you are ordering by air, realize that shedders are fragile and expensive, given their weight in water.) A Maine lobsterman we know describes shedders this way: "When you pick 'em up, there's nobody home."

Rich is one word that always seems to come to mind when we think about lobster, so we were surprised to learn that lobster is low in fat. It's also low in cholesterol, about 95 milligrams per 3½ ounces—comparable to skinless chicken. Maybe it's the ever-present pool of butter served alongside that makes us think lobster is so rich.

—JANE DANIELS LEAR

Grilled corn with cayenne butter

4 ears corn, each cut into thirds

½ stick (¼ cup) unsalted butter

2 teaspoons finely grated fresh lime zest

1 teaspoon fresh lime juice

½ teaspoon salt

½ teaspoon cayenne

Prepare grill for cooking.

Cook corn in a large pot of boiling salted water until crisp-tender, about 5 minutes, then drain in a colander. Pat dry and transfer to a large bowl.

Melt butter in a small saucepan and stir in zest, juice, salt, and cayenne. Pour three fourths of butter over corn and toss well.

Grill corn on rack set 5 to 6 inches over glowing coals, turning constantly and brushing with remaining butter, until browned on all sides, about 5 minutes.

SERVES 6

Strawberry-rhubarb parfaits

1½ lb rhubarb stalks, trimmed and cut into 1-inch pieces

2 tablespoons confectioners sugar

1 (10-oz) package thawed frozen "lite" strawberries in syrup

2 tablespoons light corn syrup

1½ pints low-fat superpremium vanilla ice cream, softened

Preheat oven to 400°F.

Arrange rhubarb in 1 layer on a lightly oiled shallow (1-inch-deep) baking pan and sprinkle with confectioners sugar. Roast in middle of oven until very tender, about 30 minutes, then cool in pan on a rack. Purée rhubarb in a blender until smooth and transfer to a bowl.

Purée strawberries and corn syrup in blender. Force purée through a fine sieve into a bowl and discard seeds. Stir one third of rhubarb purée into strawberry purée. Stir together remaining rhubarb purée and ice cream and freeze until firm enough to scoop, 1 to 2 hours.

Layer strawberry-rhubarb purée and ice-cream mixture in 6 (8-oz) stemmed glasses and serve immediately.

COOKS' NOTES

• Rhubarb may be roasted 1 day ahead, then cooled and chilled, covered.

• Rhubarb and strawberry purées may be made 1 day ahead and chilled, covered.

SERVES 6

FOR THE PRETTIEST PARFAITS, LOOK FOR THE REDDEST RHUBARB POSSIBLE.

SPLASHES OF COLOR and fresh flavor make this cookout one to be ear-marked for the height of the season. All your favorite summer harvests are here in recipes that feature inspired combinations and are a snap to prepare. Pita "nachos" topped with cheese, tomatoes, and corn, are paired with guacamole. Cucumbers blended with yellow bell peppers, jalapeños, sour cream, lime juice, and cilantro meld into a spicy cool soup. Small pieces of corn on the cob and pork tenderloin are skewered, brushed with red pepper oil, and then grilled. Even the raspberry pie—a berry purée and custard dream—is anything but ordinary.

Pork on the grill

Tomato and corn "nachos" with spicy guacamole

FOR GUACAMOLE

2 ripe California avocados

2 scallions, minced

¼ cup chopped fresh cilantro

1 tablespoon fresh lime juice

2 jalapeño chiles, seeded and minced

½ teaspoon salt

¼ teaspoon black pepper

FOR NACHOS

2 tablespoons olive oil

1 small onion, finely chopped

2 garlic cloves, minced

4 tomatoes (1¼ lb), chopped

⅔ cup fresh corn kernels (cut from 2 ears)

3 (6-inch) pita pockets, halved horizontally

1½ cups grated Pepper Jack cheese (6 oz)

MAKE GUACAMOLE:

Halve and pit avocados, then scoop flesh into a bowl. Coarsely mash with a fork, then stir in remaining guacamole ingredients.

MAKE NACHOS:

Preheat oven to 375°F.

Heat oil in a large heavy skillet over moderately low heat until hot but not smoking, then cook onion, stirring, until softened, 4 to 6 minutes. Add garlic and cook, stirring, 1 minute. Add tomatoes and corn and cook, stirring, until tomatoes are soft, 10 to 12 minutes. Season with salt and pepper.

Cut each pita half into 4 triangles, then bake in middle of oven on an ungreased baking sheet until crisp, about 8 minutes.

Preheat broiler.

Top each triangle with 1 rounded tablespoon tomato mixture and 1 tablespoon cheese, then broil 5 to 6 inches from heat until cheese melts, 2 to 3 minutes.

Serve nachos with guacamole.

MAKES 24 HORS D'OEUVRES

Creamy cucumber gazpacho

3 English cucumbers (2 lb total), peeled

1½ yellow bell peppers, cut into ¼-inch dice

1½ fresh jalapeño chiles, seeded and minced

1 large garlic clove, minced

3 tablespoons fresh lime juice

¾ cup chopped fresh cilantro

¾ cup sour cream

1 teaspoon salt

¼ teaspoon black pepper

Seed cucumbers and put seeds in a blender. Cut cucumbers into ¼-inch dice and combine with bell peppers, chiles, garlic, and lime juice in a large metal bowl. Transfer half of mixture to blender with seeds and purée until smooth. Return purée to bowl and stir in remaining ingredients. Quick-chill soup in a bowl set in a larger bowl of ice and cold water, stirring, until cold, about 20 minutes.

COOKS' NOTE

• Soup may be chilled in the refrigerator, covered, 1 to 4 hours.

MAKES ABOUT 5¼ CUPS

Corn and pork kebabs with rosemary green beans and potatoes

6 large ears corn, shucked and cut crosswise into 36 (1-inch) pieces

2 pork tenderloins (2 lb total), cut into 48 (1-inch) pieces

3 tablespoons red-wine vinegar

3 tablespoons extra-virgin olive oil

2½ teaspoons dried hot red pepper flakes

1½ teaspoons salt

¾ lb boiling potatoes

1½ lb green beans, trimmed and halved

1 tablespoon fresh rosemary, finely chopped

1 tablespoon minced garlic

Special equipment: 12 (10-inch) metal skewers

Prepare grill for cooking.

Thread 3 pieces corn and 4 pieces pork onto each skewer (see photo, right). Whisk together 2 tablespoons vinegar, 2 tablespoons oil, red pepper flakes, and salt in a small bowl, then divide between 2 small bowls (to prevent potential contamination from uncooked meat juices). Brush kebabs with red pepper oil from 1 bowl and grill on a lightly oiled rack set 5 to 6 inches over glowing coals, turning occasionally, until pork is cooked through, 15 to 20 minutes. Coat kebabs with a clean brush with red pepper oil from other bowl.

While kebabs grill, cut potatoes into ⅛-inch-thick slices and arrange in a steamer with green beans on top. Steam over boiling water, covered, until potatoes are tender, 6 to 8 minutes. Whisk together remaining tablespoon vinegar, remaining tablespoon oil, rosemary, garlic, and salt and pepper to taste in a large bowl. Add hot vegetables and toss to combine.

Serve kebabs with vegetables.

SERVES **6**

Raspberry semifreddo torte

WE USE WALKERS, A BUTTERY SHORTBREAD (FROM SCOTLAND) FOR OUR CRUST.

2 (5⅓-oz) boxes shortbread, broken into pieces

½ cup natural almonds, toasted and cooled

2 large eggs

½ cup plus 1 tablespoon sugar

1½ cups raspberries (6 oz)

1 cup chilled heavy cream

Accompaniment: mixed-berry compote (recipe follows)

Special equipment: a 9-inch (24-cm) spring-form pan

Preheat oven to 350°F.

MAKE CRUST:

Pulse shortbread with almonds in a food processor until finely ground. Press firmly over bottom and 1¼ inches up side of springform pan. Bake crust in middle of oven 10 minutes, then cool in pan on a rack.

MAKE FILLING:

Beat eggs, ½ cup sugar, and a pinch of salt in a metal bowl with a handheld electric mixer at medium-high speed until doubled in volume, about 5 minutes. Set bowl over a saucepan with 1 inch of simmering water and beat custard until an instant-read thermometer registers 140°F, about 5 minutes. Continue beating over heat 3 minutes more. Remove bowl from heat and chill custard until cool, about 10 minutes.

Toss raspberries with remaining tablespoon sugar in a large fine sieve set over a bowl, then force berries through sieve, pressing on solids, and discard seeds. Fold strained raspberries into cooled custard. Beat cream with cleaned beaters until it just holds stiff peaks, then fold gently into raspberry custard.

Spoon filling into crust, smoothing top. Wrap pan in foil and freeze at least 4 hours. (Filling will be firm but not frozen solid.)

Run a thin knife around edge of torte and remove side of pan.

COOKS' NOTE

• Torte can be frozen up to 2 days.

Photo on page 150

Mixed-berry compote

3 tablespoons unsalted butter

¼ cup packed light brown sugar

2 tablespoons fresh lemon juice

3 cups mixed berries (¾ lb) such as raspberries, blackberries, and blueberries

Melt butter in a skillet over moderate heat, then add brown sugar and lemon juice, stirring until sugar is dissolved. Add berries and cook, tossing gently (try to keep most of them from breaking up), until berries are warm and juices begin to be released, 2 to 3 minutes. Serve warm or at room temperature.

COOKS' NOTE

• This compote also tastes great over ice cream or pound cake.

MAKES ABOUT 3 CUPS

Chicken on the grill

THE SIMPLEST COOKOUTS, like

this one, are those with lots of marinated

dishes. Here, the chickens are halved,

marinated for a day in an herbal vinai-

grette laced with hot red pepper flakes,

then grilled to golden brown perfection.

The result is tender meat infused with

lemon, garlic, rosemary, and thyme

that's further enhanced with unbeatable

charcoal flavor. Dessert is pretty and

luscious—blueberry-lemon tartlets kissed

with sweetened whipped cream.

Red-leaf lettuce with shallot vinaigrette

1 large shallot, minced

2 teaspoons white-wine vinegar

2 teaspoons Dijon mustard

3½ tablespoons olive oil

Kosher salt to taste

1 large head red-leaf lettuce, torn into bite-size pieces

Stir together shallot and vinegar and let stand 10 minutes. Whisk in mustard, oil, kosher salt, and pepper to taste until blended.

Toss lettuce with vinaigrette.

COOKS' NOTE

• You can wash lettuce a day ahead—wrap it in paper towels, then chill in plastic bags.

SERVES 4

Grilled lemon-herb marinated chicken

NEW YORK CHEF MARK STRAUSMAN CREATED THIS RECIPE— DELICIOUS, SIMPLE, AND LOW FAT.

2 whole chickens (preferably organic; 2 lb each)

6 garlic cloves, minced

12 fresh rosemary sprigs

12 fresh thyme sprigs

½ cup fresh lemon juice

2 tablespoons balsamic vinegar

1 tablespoon extra-virgin olive oil

4 teaspoons dried hot red pepper flakes

2 teaspoons fresh oregano

Garnish: fresh rosemary and thyme sprigs

Cut out backbone of each chicken with poultry shears and discard. Cut off first 2 wing joints from each chicken and discard. Halve chickens lengthwise and discard skin. Put chickens in a large bowl with remaining ingredients and salt to taste and turn chickens to coat. Marinate chickens, covered and chilled, turning occasionally, 1 day.

Prepare grill for cooking.

Discard marinade and season chickens with salt and pepper. Grill chickens on a lightly oiled rack set 5 to 6 inches over glowing coals, turning occasionally, until cooked through, about 30 minutes.

COOKS' NOTE:

• Alternatively, you can grill the chickens in 2 batches in a hot lightly oiled well-seasoned ridged grill pan over moderate heat.

SERVES 4

Grilled balsamic-marinated eggplant

2½ tablespoons balsamic vinegar

½ tablespoon packed dark brown sugar

1 garlic clove, minced

2½ tablespoons olive oil

4 small eggplants (1½ lb), cut crosswise into ½-inch-thick rounds

2 tablespoons thinly sliced fresh basil

Prepare grill for cooking.

Stir together vinegar, sugar, garlic, and oil in a shallow glass baking dish. Add eggplant rounds and marinate, turning once, 10 minutes. Drain, reserving marinade.

Grill eggplant on an oiled rack set 5 to 6 inches over glowing coals, basting constantly with reserved marinade and turning once, until browned and tender on both sides, about 10 minutes. Transfer to a platter and season with salt and pepper. Chill, covered, 30 minutes.

Just before serving, sprinkle with basil.

SERVES 4

Grilled yellow squash and orzo salad

1 small yellow squash, cut lengthwise into ½-inch-thick slices

1 small zucchini, cut lengthwise into ½-inch-thick slices

1 red bell pepper, sides removed (see box on page 25)

3 tablespoons olive oil

2 tablespoons fresh orange juice

1 tablespoon fresh lemon juice

1 small garlic clove, minced

½ lb orzo (1 cup)

1 tomato, chopped

⅓ cup chopped fresh flat-leaf parsley

Prepare grill for cooking.

Brush yellow squash, zucchini, and red pepper with 1 tablespoon oil and season with salt and pepper. Grill vegetables on a rack set 5 to 6 inches over glowing coals, turning once, until golden on both sides, 6 to 7 minutes. Chop vegetables into ½-inch pieces.

Stir together orange juice, lemon juice, garlic, and remaining 2 tablespoons oil in a small bowl.

Cook orzo in a large pot of boiling salted water until tender. Drain in a colander, then toss with grilled vegetables, tomato, parsley, and salt and pepper to taste. Chill, covered, 30 minutes.

SERVES 4

Blueberry-lemon tartlets with gingersnap crusts

20 gingersnap cookies, finely ground in a food processor (about 1 cup)

½ stick (¼ cup) unsalted butter, melted and cooled

1 tablespoon cornstarch

1 tablespoon water

1 lemon

2 cups blueberries

½ cup sugar

¼ cup heavy cream

1 tablespoon confectioners sugar

Special equipment: 4 (3- by ¾-inch) tartlet pans

Stir together gingersnap crumbs and butter until combined well, then press one fourth of mixture firmly onto bottom and up sides of each tartlet pan. Refrigerate until firm, about 30 minutes.

Stir together cornstarch and water in a small bowl. Peel a 3- by ½-inch strip of zest from lemon, reserving lemon. Boil blueberries, sugar, cornstarch mixture, and lemon strip in a small heavy saucepan, stirring, until thickened, about 3 minutes. Transfer to a bowl, then cover and cool to room temperature.

Preheat oven to 375°F.

Bake tartlet shells on a baking sheet in middle of oven until edges are golden, about 8 minutes. Cool shells in pans on a wire rack 10 minutes, then remove shells from pans (if necessary, use tip of a sharp knife to ease shell out of pan) and cool completely.

Finely grate enough zest from reserved lemon to measure ½ teaspoon. Beat cream with confectioners sugar until it just holds soft peaks and gently stir in zest.

Spoon blueberry filling into shells and top each with a dollop of whipped cream.

COOKS' NOTE

• Tartlet shells can be baked 1 day ahead and kept at room temperature, covered.

MAKES **4** TARTLETS

Fresh from the sea grill

THERE ARE TIMES during the steamy months when a salad is just about all you want for dinner. Should you find yourself entertaining on such an evening, this little menu, featuring a salad from the sea, is ideal. Here you have the option of squid or shrimp, so you might want to find out your guests' preferences in advance or go ahead and prepare both (just remember to double the spice mixture for coating). Caipirinhas, favorite Brazilian cocktails, are served icy-cold; peach-almond granita makes a cooling finale.

Caipirinhas

THIS DRINK'S PRIMARY INGREDIENT, CACHAÇA, IS AN AGUARDIENTE THAT, LIKE RUM, IS MADE FROM SUGARCANE.

15 limes

½ cup superfine granulated sugar

1½ cups cachaça

Garnish: lime wedges and/or sugarcane sticks

Squeeze enough juice from limes to measure 2 cups, then stir together with sugar in a pitcher until sugar is dissolved. Add ice cubes and cachaça, stirring until combined well.

COOKS' NOTES:

• A Caipirinha is usually made by muddling pieces of lime with sugar; we chose, for simplicity's sake, to juice the limes instead. For a more authentic flavor, you can mash a piece of lime rind in the bottom of the glass before serving.

• You can substitute equal parts white rum and white tequila in place of the cachaça.

MAKES **8** DRINKS

Grilled polenta cakes with tomato-olive salsa

2 tablespoons olive oil

1 small onion, finely chopped

2 garlic cloves, minced

2 tomatoes, chopped

¼ cup Kalamata or other brine-cured black olives, pitted and chopped

½ lb store-bought plain polenta roll (from a 1-lb package), trimmed and cut into 8 (⅓-inch-thick) slices

3 tablespoons freshly grated parmesan

1 tablespoon chopped fresh thyme

Prepare grill for cooking.

Heat 1 tablespoon oil in a skillet over moderately high heat until hot but not smoking, then cook onion, stirring, until golden brown, about 6 minutes. Add garlic and cook, stirring, 1 minute. Add tomatoes and salt and pepper to taste and cook, stirring occasionally, until tomatoes are soft, 6 to 8 minutes. Remove from heat and stir in olives.

Brush both sides of polenta slices with remaining tablespoon olive oil. Grill on an oiled rack set 5 to 6 inches over glowing coals until undersides are golden, 3 to 4 minutes. Turn slices over and top evenly with cheese. Grill until undersides are golden, about 2 minutes more. Transfer to a platter and top with tomato mixture, then sprinkle with thyme.

SERVES **4**

Grilled squid on spinach, red pepper, and mango salad

THIS SALAD
ALSO CAN BE
MADE WITH
GRILLED
SHRIMP, WHICH
IS EQUALLY
DELICIOUS.

1½ lb cleaned small squid or 1½ lb large shrimp (about 25), shelled and deveined

1½ teaspoons chili powder

1 teaspoon ground cumin

¼ teaspoon cayenne

¼ cup plus 2 teaspoons extra-virgin olive oil

2 red bell peppers

10 oz baby spinach, trimmed (6 cups)

1 mango, peeled, pitted, and cut into ½-inch cubes (2 cups)

½ small red onion, sliced

2 tablespoons fresh lime juice plus 8 lime wedges

Prepare grill for cooking.

Cut squid bodies open to make flat pieces and score inner sides of flattened squids in a cross-hatch pattern with a sharp knife, blade held horizontally at a 30-degree angle (do not cut all the way through flesh). Pat squid bodies and tentacles (or shrimp) dry and toss with spices and 1 teaspoon oil.

Cut sides from bell peppers (see box on page 25) and brush with 1 teaspoon oil.

Grill bell peppers on a lightly oiled rack set 5 to 6 inches over glowing coals, turning once, until just tender, about 4 minutes. Cut bell peppers into strips. Grill squid bodies, crosshatch sides down, and tentacles, turning once, until just cooked through (squid will curl up as it cooks), about 2 minutes (or 2 minutes per side if cooking shrimp).

Toss together bell peppers, spinach, mango, onion, lime juice, remaining ¼ cup oil, and salt and pepper to taste.

Top salad with squid (or shrimp) and serve with lime wedges.

SERVES 4

Peach-almond granita

½ cup water

¼ cup sugar

3 large peaches (1½ lb), peeled and thinly sliced

1½ tablespoons Di Saronno Amaretto or other almond-flavored liqueur

⅛ teaspoon salt

Bring water and sugar to a boil, stirring until sugar is dissolved. Boil 1 minute, then cool slightly.

Purée peaches in a food processor until smooth, then blend in sugar syrup, liqueur, and salt. Transfer to a 9-inch metal baking pan and freeze, covered with plastic wrap, until almost frozen, about 2 hours. Scrape ice with a fork to separate. Freeze 2 hours more, then scrape ice in same manner. Spoon into glasses.

COOKS' NOTE

• Granita can be made 1 day ahead. Let stand at room temperature 10 minutes, then scrape before serving.

SERVES 4

PICNICS REMIND US of long carefree summers. No matter our age, there's something irresistible about laying out a blanket, wiggling our toes in the grass (or sand), and munching on snacks. Since the water holds endless appeal when the weather turns sultry, we've created a picnic for the beach and another for the lake. You'll find wonderful spreads for the cooler months as well.

Easy picnics

Picnic at the beach

THE NEXT TIME the forecast promises a perfect beach day, head to the shore with a few friends, some comfortable sand chairs, and a cooler packed with goodies. The plan is to enjoy this picnic later in the day, after hours in the sun and surf. You'll begin with Southsides—lemon gin cocktails—and an addictive spicy party mix. Then, after cocktail hour, tuna and olive sandwiches, crunchy watercress salad, and big chocolate-chunk cookies will make onlookers jealous. Not to worry, you'll have more than enough cookies to share if you want more company.

Picnic at the beach

THE NEXT TIME the forecast promises a perfect beach day, head to the shore with a few friends, some comfortable sand chairs, and a cooler packed with goodies. The plan is to enjoy this picnic later in the day, after hours in the sun and surf. You'll begin with Southsides—lemon gin cocktails—and an addictive spicy party mix. Then, after cocktail hour, tuna and olive sandwiches, crunchy watercress salad, and big chocolate-chunk cookies will make onlookers jealous. Not to worry, you'll have more than enough cookies to share if you want more company.

Easy picnics

Southsides

Lemon gin cocktails

1 cup water

1 cup sugar

1⅓ cups fresh lemon juice

¼ cup packed fresh mint

6 oz gin, vodka, or rum, or to taste

Seltzer or club soda (optional)

Bring water and sugar to a boil in a small saucepan, stirring, until sugar is completely dissolved. Cool syrup.

Blend ⅔ cup syrup, lemon juice, and mint in a blender until completely smooth, then add additional syrup to taste.

Fill 4 glasses with ice and add liquor and lemon mixture. Top off with seltzer.

COOKS' NOTES

• Syrup may be made 2 weeks ahead and chilled, covered.

• Lemon mixture may be made 4 hours ahead and chilled in an airtight container.

MAKES 4 DRINKS

Spicy crunch mix

2 cups vegetable oil

6 large shallots (½ lb), cut crosswise into ¼-inch-thick slices

¼ teaspoon cayenne, or to taste

½ teaspoon ground cumin

1 cup unseasoned freeze-dried peas

1 cup unseasoned dry-roasted soybeans

Heat oil in a deep 12-inch heavy skillet over moderately high heat until hot but not smoking, then fry shallots, stirring occasionally, until golden brown, about 7 minutes. Transfer to paper towels with a slotted spoon to drain and season with salt. Pour off all but about 1½ tablespoons oil from skillet, then stir in cayenne and cumin. Cook spices over moderate heat, stirring, until fragrant, about 10 seconds. Remove skillet from heat and cool seasoned oil to room temperature.

Add shallots, peas, soybeans, and salt and pepper to taste to seasoned oil, tossing to coat.

COOKS' NOTES

• Freeze-dried peas and dry-roasted soybeans are available at specialty foods shops and some natural foods stores and supermarkets and by mail order from Just Tomatoes, (800) 537-1985.

• Mix may be made 1 day ahead and kept in an airtight container at room temperature.

MAKES ABOUT 3 CUPS

Tuna and olive salad sandwiches

¼ cup mayonnaise

2 tablespoons fresh lemon juice

2 (6-oz) cans light tuna packed in olive oil, drained

½ cup chopped drained bottled roasted red peppers

10 Kalamata or other brine-cured black olives, pitted and cut lengthwise into strips

1 large celery rib, chopped

2 tablespoons finely chopped red onion

1 (20- to 24-inch) baguette

2 tablespoons olive oil

Green-leaf lettuce

Whisk together mayonnaise and lemon juice in a large bowl. Add tuna, roasted peppers, olives, celery, and onion and stir together gently. Season with salt and pepper.

Cut baguette into 4 equal lengths and halve each piece horizontally. Brush cut sides with oil and season with salt and pepper. Make sandwiches with baguette, tuna salad, and lettuce.

SERVES 4

Chopped watercress salad with cucumber and sesame seeds

1½ tablespoons rice vinegar

½ teaspoon sugar

½ teaspoon salt

1½ tablespoons vegetable oil

1 English cucumber, peeled, seeded, and diced

1 yellow bell pepper, cut into ½-inch dice

1 small red onion, cut into ½-inch dice

3 bunches watercress (1 lb), tough stems trimmed and sprigs coarsely chopped

2 tablespoons sesame seeds, toasted and cooled

Whisk together vinegar, sugar, and salt in a large bowl. Whisk in oil, then season with pepper. Add cucumber, bell pepper, and onion and let stand 5 minutes.

Add watercress and toss well. Season with salt and pepper and sprinkle with sesame seeds.

SERVES 4

Chocolate-chunk oatmeal coconut cookies

2 sticks (1 cup) unsalted butter, softened

1 cup packed brown sugar

6 tablespoons granulated sugar

2 large eggs

1½ teaspoons vanilla

½ teaspoon baking soda

½ teaspoon salt

1 cup all-purpose flour

2¼ cups old-fashioned oats

1½ cups finely shredded unsweetened dried coconut

12 oz semisweet or bittersweet (not unsweetened) ½-inch chocolate chunks (2 cups)

¾ cup almonds with skins (4 oz), toasted, cooled, and chopped

Preheat oven to 375°F.

Beat together butter and sugars in a bowl with an electric mixer at high speed until fluffy. Add eggs and beat until just blended, then beat in vanilla, baking soda, and salt. Add flour and mix at low speed until just blended. Stir in oats, coconut, chocolate, and almonds.

Drop ¼ cup dough for each cookie onto 2 large lightly buttered baking sheets, about 3 inches apart (about 8 cookies per sheet), then gently pat down each mound to about ½ inch thick. Bake in upper and lower thirds of oven, switching position of and rotating pans halfway through baking, until golden, 15 to 18 minutes total.

Cool cookies on sheets 1 minute, then transfer with a spatula to racks to cool completely. Make more cookies in same manner.

COOKS' NOTE

• A good way to get large chunks of chocolate for these cookies is to coarsely chop a 1-pound block of semisweet chocolate into ½-inch pieces. Weigh the pieces, then save the fine powdery chocolate for another recipe that calls for melted chocolate.

MAKES ABOUT 2 DOZEN LARGE COOKIES

Lunchbox picnic

WHEN YOU WANT to impress your
friends with a picnic *extraordinaire*, choose
this one. The summer rolls, so chic to
serve away from home, crunch with fresh-
ness. They can be made a day in advance
and transported easily (just be sure to
wrap them individually in plastic wrap to
keep them moist). Then, too, there is a
choice of sandwiches— minted lobster
salad or sesame chicken. Both are exceptional; either is delicious with the green
beans in garlic sauce. Be sure to pack
everything into a cooler (including the
lunchboxes) along with some nice
cool drinks.

Vegetable summer rolls

¼ cup sugar

3 tablespoons Asian fish sauce

2 tablespoons fresh lime juice

1 tablespoon distilled white vinegar

1 teaspoon minced garlic

¼ teaspoon dried hot red pepper flakes

FOR ROLLS

3 medium portobello mushroom caps, stems discarded

2 tablespoons vegetable oil

12 (8-inch) rice-paper rounds plus extra (in case of tearing)

1 English cucumber, peeled, seeded, and cut into 3-inch julienne strips

2 carrots, cut into 3-inch julienne strips

1 red bell pepper, cut into 3-inch julienne strips

1 bunch chives, cut into 3-inch lengths

1 bunch cilantro, tough stems discarded

1 cup fresh mint

¼ cup unsalted dry-roasted peanuts, chopped

MAKE SAUCE:

Whisk together sauce ingredients until sugar is dissolved.

MAKE ROLLS:

Brush mushroom caps with oil and season with salt and pepper. Cook in a well-seasoned ridged grill pan or large heavy skillet over moderately high heat, turning occasionally, until browned and tender, about 10 minutes. Cool, then thinly slice.

Gently immerse 1 rice-paper round in a large bowl of warm water and let stand until softened, about 1 minute. Carefully lay round on paper towels, then blot to remove excess moisture. Arrange several pieces of mushrooms, cucumber, carrots, bell pepper, and chive in a pile in center of round. Top with some cilantro and mint and sprinkle with some peanuts. Fold 1 edge of wrapper over filling, fold in sides, then carefully roll up toward open edge. Make more rolls in same manner.

Serve rolls with dipping sauce.

COOKS' NOTE

• Rolls can be made 1 day ahead, wrapped individually in plastic wrap and chilled, covered.

MAKES 12 ROLLS

Green beans in garlic sauce

¾ lb green beans, trimmed

1 tablespoon minced garlic

2 tablespoons vegetable oil

2 tablespoons soy sauce

1 tablespoon oyster sauce

½ tablespoon rice vinegar

½ teaspoon dried hot red pepper flakes

Cook beans in boiling salted water until crisp-tender, about 5 minutes. Drain and rinse under cold running water, then pat dry.

Cook garlic in oil in a large skillet over moderate heat, stirring, until fragrant and just beginning to color, 1 to 2 minutes. Remove from heat and whisk in remaining ingredients. Add beans, tossing to coat well. Serve at room temperature.

SERVES 4

Sesame chicken with napa cabbage and spinach slaw on baguette

1½ tablespoons all-purpose flour

2 tablespoons sesame seeds

1 large egg white

1 teaspoon water

2 small boneless skinless whole chicken breasts (1 lb total), halved and flattened slightly

2 teaspoons Asian sesame oil

1 tablespoon fresh lemon juice

1 (20-inch) baguette, cut crosswise into 4 pieces

4 cups shredded Napa cabbage

2 cups packed trimmed spinach leaves, shredded

1 carrot, shredded

Put flour and sesame seeds on separate sheets of wax paper. Beat together egg white and water in a shallow bowl.

Season chicken breasts with salt and dip 1 at a time in flour, shaking off excess. Dip chicken in egg white, letting excess drip off, then coat with sesame seeds on 1 side, shaking off excess. Transfer as coated to a plate.

Heat 1 teaspoon oil in a large nonstick skillet over moderate heat until hot but not smoking, then cook chicken, seeded sides down, until golden, about 4 minutes. Turn chicken over and cook until just cooked through, about 4 minutes more. Add lemon juice, then turn chicken to coat with juice and cook until juice is almost evaporated, about 1 minute. Transfer chicken to a cutting board and halve lengthwise.

Make a horizontal cut through center of each baguette piece with a serrated knife, cutting almost but not all the way through, then spread open. Toss cabbage, spinach, and carrot with remaining teaspoon oil and salt to taste in a bowl.

Make sandwiches with slaw, chicken, and bread.

MAKES **4** SANDWICHES

Minted lobster salad in pitas

4 (6-inch) pita pockets

2 tablespoons low-fat mayonnaise

1 tablespoon fresh lemon juice

¾ teaspoon finely grated fresh orange zest

½ teaspoon anise seeds, crushed with a mortar and pestle or bottom of a heavy skillet

⅛ teaspoon cayenne

1 medium fennel bulb (sometimes called anise; 1 lb), stalks trimmed flush with bulb and bulb cut into very thin slices

¾ lb cooked lobster meat, chopped

2 cups shredded romaine

¼ cup fresh mint, coarsely chopped

Preheat oven to 350°F.

Cut off one fourth of each pita pocket and reserve larger portions of pitas wrapped in plastic wrap. Chop smaller portions into ½-inch pieces, then toast in a shallow baking pan in middle of oven until golden, about 7 minutes.

Stir together mayonnaise, juice, zest, anise seeds, and cayenne in a bowl. Add fennel, lobster, romaine, mint, and pita croutons and toss to coat. Fill reserved pitas with lobster salad.

MAKES **4** SANDWICHES

Photo on page 168

Individual blueberry-coconut pound cakes

1 stick (½ cup) unsalted butter, softened

¾ cup sugar

2 teaspoons finely grated fresh lime zest

2 large eggs

5 tablespoons heavy cream

1 cup all-purpose flour

¼ teaspoon salt

½ cup plus 3 tablespoons sweetened flaked coconut

½ cup blueberries

Preheat oven to 350°F. Butter and flour 9 (½–cup) muffin cups (just butter if nonstick).

Beat together butter, sugar, and zest until light and fluffy, then beat in eggs 1 at a time. Beat in cream, then flour and salt, at low speed until just combined. Stir in ½ cup coconut and gently stir in blueberries. Spoon batter into muffin cups and smooth tops. Sprinkle tops with remaining 3 tablespoons coconut.

Bake in middle of oven until a tester comes out clean and edges are golden brown, about 25 minutes. Invert onto a rack and cool.

SERVES **4**

Picnic at the lake

AFTER A DAY OF SWIMMING and
boating, everyone's bound to be famished,
and you'll want to have a substantial meal
on hand. Here's a picnic that will appeal
to kids and adults alike, and will fill them
to the brim. Who, after all, doesn't like
creamy onion dip, roasted chicken, rice
salad, and a choice of three dessert bars—
lemon, chocolate, and pecan? Our original
thought was to offer the bar cookie
variations as optional, but now it seems
like a very good idea to make at least two
different kinds.

Caramelized onion and roasted red pepper dip

1 red bell pepper

2 tablespoons extra-virgin olive oil

2 onions, chopped

6 oz cream cheese, softened

¾ cup sour cream

1 teaspoon kosher salt

2 scallions, finely chopped

Accompaniments: celery and carrot sticks and potato chips

Lay red bell pepper on its side on rack of a gas burner and turn flame on high (or put pepper on rack of broiler about 2 inches from heat). Roast pepper, turning with tongs, until skin is blackened, 5 to 8 minutes. Transfer to a bowl and let stand, covered with plastic wrap, 15 minutes.

Heat olive oil in a heavy skillet over high heat until hot but not smoking, then cook onions, without stirring, until beginning to caramelize, about 2 minutes. Reduce heat to moderate and cook, stirring, until onions are softened and caramelized, about 5 minutes. Transfer to paper towels to drain.

Peel pepper, then discard seeds and ribs and finely dice flesh. Whisk together cream cheese, sour cream, and salt in a bowl, then stir in bell pepper, caramelized onion, and pepper to taste. Stir in scallions just before serving.

COOKS' NOTE

• Dip can be made (without scallions) 1 day ahead and chilled, covered. Stir in scallions just before serving.

MAKES ABOUT 2¼ CUPS

Roasted chicken with prosciutto and basil

1 (6- to 8-lb) chicken, cut into 8 pieces, wings split, and breasts and thighs halved crosswise

¼ lb thinly sliced prosciutto, torn into small pieces

About 14 large basil leaves

Preheat oven to 400°F.

Loosen skin from chicken pieces except wings, leaving skin attached on 1 or 2 sides. Working with 1 piece of chicken at a time, lift skin up and lay prosciutto and basil on meat, then smooth skin back into place. Season chicken with salt and pepper and arrange in a large shallow baking pan. Roast in middle of oven until chicken is cooked through, 30 to 40 minutes.

Preheat broiler.

Broil chicken 3 inches from heat until skin is browned, about 2 minutes. Serve warm or at room temperature.

COOKS' NOTE

• Chicken can be cooked 4 hours ahead. Cool before wrapping.

SERVES 6

Lemony rice salad with peas and mint

2 cups Arborio rice

1 (10-oz) package frozen baby peas, thawed

¼ cup extra-virgin olive oil

1½ tablespoons fresh lemon juice

1 teaspoon finely grated fresh lemon zest

1 teaspoon kosher salt, or to taste

½ teaspoon black pepper

⅓ cup torn fresh mint leaves

Cook rice in a large pot of boiling salted water, stirring, until just tender, about 14 minutes. Drain in a colander and rinse under cold water, then drain well. Transfer to a large bowl and add peas.

Whisk together oil, lemon juice, zest, salt, and pepper, then toss with rice and peas. Just before serving, sprinkle with mint and toss again.

COOKS' NOTE

• Rice salad can be made (without mint) 1 day ahead and chilled, covered. Stir in mint just before serving.

SERVES 6

Pecan-pie bars

Hot shortbread base (recipe on page 176)

8 oz pecans (2 cups)

1 stick (½ cup) unsalted butter

1 cup packed light brown sugar

⅓ cup honey

2 tablespoons heavy cream

Prepare topping while shortbread bakes:

Coarsely chop pecans in a food processor. Melt butter in a heavy saucepan, then stir in brown sugar, honey, and cream. Simmer, stirring occasionally, 1 minute, then stir in pecans. Pour pecan topping over hot shortbread and spread evenly. Bake in middle of oven until bubbling, about 20 minutes. Cool completely in pan and cut into 24 bars.

COOKS' NOTE

• Bar cookies keep, covered, 5 days at room temperature.

MAKES 24 BARS

Photo on page 177

OUR BAR TREATS ARE ALL BUILT UPON A HOT SHORTBREAD FOUNDATION. BE SURE YOUR CHOSEN TOPPING IS PREPARED WHILE THE SHORTBREAD BAKES.

Shortbread base

1½ sticks (¾ cup) unsalted butter, cut into ½-inch pieces

2 cups all-purpose flour

½ cup packed light brown sugar

½ teaspoon salt

Preheat oven to 350°F.

Process all ingredients in a food processor until mixture begins to form small lumps. Sprinkle into a 13- by 9- by 2-inch baking pan and press evenly onto bottom with a metal spatula. Bake shortbread in middle of oven until golden, about 20 minutes.

Fudgy brownie bars

Hot shortbread base (recipe above)

8 oz bittersweet chocolate (not unsweetened), coarsely chopped

2 sticks (1 cup) unsalted butter

1½ cups sugar

4 large eggs

¾ cup all-purpose flour

¼ teaspoon salt

Prepare topping while shortbread bakes:

Melt chocolate with butter in a small saucepan over moderately low heat, stirring until smooth. Remove from heat and stir in sugar. Add eggs, beating with a fork until incorporated, then stir in flour and salt.

Pour chocolate topping over hot shortbread and spread evenly. Bake in middle of oven until a tester comes out with crumbs adhering, about 35 minutes. Cool completely in pan and cut into 24 bars.

COOKS' NOTE

• Bar cookies keep, covered, 5 days at room temperature.

MAKES **24** BARS

Lemon bars

Hot shortbread base (recipe on this page)

4 large eggs

1½ cups granulated sugar

¾ cup fresh lemon juice

⅓ cup all-purpose flour

3 tablespoons confectioners sugar

Prepare topping while shortbread bakes:

Whisk together eggs and granulated sugar in a bowl, then stir in lemon juice and flour.

Pour lemon topping over hot shortbread. Reduce oven temperature to 300°F and bake in middle of oven until set, about 30 minutes. Cool completely in pan and cut into 24 bars.

Sift confectioners sugar over bars before serving.

COOKS' NOTE

• Bar cookies keep, covered and chilled, 3 days.

MAKES **24** BARS

Apple orchard picnic

WHETHER YOU'RE GOING to pick apples or just venturing out on a Sunday drive to view the autumn leaves, you'll be happy to have this luscious little meal in your basket. Find a dry place with a beautiful view, unfold your blanket, and set out the feast—homemade hazelnut crackers with Stilton and figs, tortilla Española, and a fresh mesclun salad with apple-maple vinaigrette. And, of course, be sure to give the wine a few minutes to breathe. You'll probably want to save the orange loaf cake for later in the afternoon. Don't forget to bring along a thermos of coffee or tea to serve with it, just before you (reluctantly) head home.

Hazelnut crackers with stilton and fresh figs

1 cup hazelnuts (4½ oz), lightly toasted and skinned (procedure follows)

1 cup all-purpose flour

⅓ cup freshly grated parmesan

1½ teaspoons salt

1½ teaspoons sugar

5 tablespoons cold unsalted butter, cut into pieces

1 large egg, lightly beaten

3 tablespoons heavy cream

Accompaniments: fresh figs and Stilton

Grind nuts in a food processor until they become a nut butter.

Whisk together flour, parmesan, salt, and sugar in a bowl. Blend in butter with a pastry blender or your fingertips until mixture resembles coarse meal. Stir in nut butter, egg, and cream until mixture just forms a dough (dough will be sticky). Knead dough on a lightly floured surface with floured hands until just smooth.

Divide dough in half and form each half into a 9- by 1½-inch log. Freeze, wrapped separately in wax paper, until firm, at least 1 hour.

Preheat oven to 400°F.

Cut logs diagonally into ⅓-inch-thick slices. Arrange slices ½ inch apart on 2 baking sheets and bake in batches in middle of oven until undersides are just golden brown, about 12 minutes. Carefully turn crackers over with a metal spatula and bake until undersides are just golden brown, about 2 minutes more. Transfer with spatula to a rack (crackers will crisp as they cool) and sprinkle lightly with salt to taste.

COOKS' NOTE

• Dough logs may be frozen up to 2 days. Let dough stand at room temperature 15 minutes before proceeding to facilitate slicing.

SERVES 6

To toast and skin hazelnuts

Preheat oven to 350°F.

Toast hazelnuts in 1 layer in a shallow baking pan in middle of oven until lightly colored and skins are blistered, 10 to 15 minutes. Wrap in a kitchen towel and let steam 1 minute. Rub nuts in towel to remove loose skins (not all skins will come off), then cool.

Tortilla española

MARÍA DE LOS ANGELES RODRÍGUEZ ARTACHO OF BAR JORDI IN BARCELONA WAS KIND ENOUGH TO SHARE HER RECIPE.

1½ cups olive oil

2½ lb boiling potatoes, peeled and cut into ⅓-inch dice

2½ cups chopped onion

1 tablespoon kosher salt

10 large eggs

Heat olive oil in a 12-inch nonstick skillet over moderate heat until hot but not smoking, then add potatoes, onion, and half of salt. Cook over moderately low heat, stirring occasionally, until vegetables are very tender but not browned, about 45 minutes. Drain in a large colander set over a bowl, reserving oil, and cool 5 minutes. Lightly beat eggs in a large bowl, then gently stir in vegetables, 1 tablespoon reserved oil, re-maining salt, and pepper to taste.

Return 1 tablespoon reserved oil to skillet and add vegetable mixture, pressing potatoes flush with eggs. Cook over low heat, covered, until almost set, 12 to 15 minutes. Turn off heat and let stand, covered, 15 minutes. Shake skillet gen-tly to make sure tortilla is set on bottom and not sticking to skillet. Invert tortilla onto a large flat plate and slide back into skillet, bottom side up. (Alternatively—especially if top is still loose at this point—slide tortilla onto plate first. Cover it with skillet and invert tortilla back into skillet.) Round edge with a rubber spatula and cook over low heat, covered, until set, about 15 minutes more. Slide tortilla onto a serving plate and serve warm or at room temperature.

COOKS' NOTE
• Tortilla keeps, covered and chilled, 2 days.

SERVES 6

Baby greens with apple-maple vinaigrette

¼ cup olive oil

1½ tablespoons cider vinegar

1½ tablespoons pure maple syrup

½ tablespoon chopped fresh tarragon

1 teaspoon coarse-grained mustard

½ teaspoon salt

1 Golden Delicious or Fuji apple, cored and cut into matchsticks

½ lb mesclun (mixed baby salad greens)

Shake oil, vinegar, syrup, tarragon, mustard, salt, and pepper to taste in a tightly closed jar. Add apple and shake again.

Put greens in a large bowl and toss with dressing just before serving.

SERVES 6

Orange tea cake

THIS CAKE
IS EVEN
BETTER IF
MADE A
DAY OR
TWO AHEAD.

1½ cups all-purpose flour

1 tablespoon finely grated fresh orange zest

1 teaspoon baking powder

½ teaspoon salt

1½ sticks (¾ cup) unsalted butter, softened

1½ cups plus ⅓ cup sugar

4 large eggs

1 large egg yolk

3 tablespoons whole milk

1 teaspoon vanilla

½ cup plus 3 tablespoons fresh orange juice

Preheat oven to 350°F. Butter a 9- by 5-inch loaf pan and line pan with a sheet of wax paper, letting paper hang over long sides by 2 inches. Butter paper.

Whisk together flour, zest, baking powder, and salt in a small bowl.

Beat together butter and 1½ cups sugar with an electric mixer at high speed until light and fluffy, then add whole eggs and yolk 1 at a time, beating well after each addition. Beat in milk and vanilla at medium speed. Add flour mixture and mix at low speed until just blended, then add 3 tablespoons orange juice and mix until batter is smooth. Pour into loaf pan, smoothing top, and bake in lower third of oven until a tester inserted in center comes out clean, about 1 hour. Cool cake in pan on a rack 5 minutes.

MAKE GLAZE WHILE CAKE BAKES:

Whisk together remaining ½ cup orange juice and remaining ⅓ cup sugar in a small bowl until sugar is dissolved.

Prick cake at ¾-inch intervals with a wooden skewer, pushing all the way through to bottom of pan. Lift cake out of pan using wax paper and transfer to rack, leaving paper on cake.

Brush one fourth of glaze over cake and let stand 5 minutes (for cake to absorb glaze). Repeat brushing 3 more times. Cool cake completely before removing paper.

COOKS' NOTE

• Cake can be made 4 days ahead and kept at room temperature, wrapped in foil.

Tailgate lunch

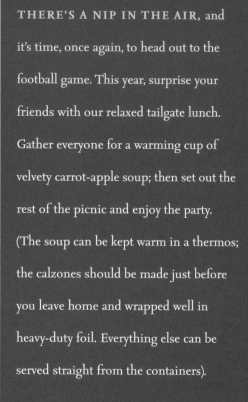

THERE'S A NIP IN THE AIR, and it's time, once again, to head out to the football game. This year, surprise your friends with our relaxed tailgate lunch. Gather everyone for a warming cup of velvety carrot-apple soup; then set out the rest of the picnic and enjoy the party. (The soup can be kept warm in a thermos; the calzones should be made just before you leave home and wrapped well in heavy-duty foil. Everything else can be served straight from the containers).

Carrot-apple soup with ginger

1 large onion, chopped

1 tablespoon olive oil

1½ lb carrots, peeled and thinly sliced

1 Granny Smith apple, peeled, cored, and chopped

2 tablespoons coarsely chopped peeled fresh ginger

4 cups water

½ cup chicken broth

1½ teaspoons kosher salt

Cook onion in oil in a 3- to 4-quart saucepan over moderate heat, stirring, until softened. Add remaining ingredients and bring to a boil. Reduce heat and simmer, partially covered, until carrots and apple are very tender, 20 to 25 minutes. Purée soup in a blender or food processor (use caution when blending hot liquids) and return to saucepan. Add additional water to thin to desired consistency. Serve warm or at room temperature.

COOKS' NOTE

• To serve the soup warm, keep it in a thermos.

MAKES ABOUT **6 CUPS**

Mini swiss-chard calzones

½ small onion, minced

1 large garlic clove, minced

2½ tablespoons extra-virgin olive oil

1 small bunch green Swiss chard (¾ lb), stems thinly sliced and leaves chopped

1 cup coarsely grated Italian Fontina cheese (4 oz)

1 lb frozen pizza or bread dough, thawed

Preheat oven to 450°F.

Cook onion and garlic in 1 tablespoon oil in a large skillet over moderate heat, stirring, until softened. Add chard stems and cook, stirring, 2 minutes. Add leaves with any water clinging to leaves and salt and pepper to taste and cook, stirring occasionally, until tender, 6 to 8 minutes. Cool to room temperature, then stir in cheese.

Divide dough into 16 pieces and cover with a kitchen towel or plastic wrap. Roll out 1 piece of dough (keep remaining dough covered) into a 4-inch round on a lightly floured surface, stretching dough with fingers if necessary. Put 1 rounded tablespoon chard filling onto one half of round, then fold other half of dough over filling. Pinch together edge of dough, then fold edge up and crimp to seal. Make more calzones in same manner, transferring as formed to a large oiled baking sheet. Brush calzones with remaining 1½ tablespoons oil and cut a small steam vent in top of each.

Bake on bottom rack of oven until golden and steaming hot, 15 to 20 minutes. Cool slightly.

MAKES **16 SMALL CALZONES**

Buffalo chicken wings

FRANK AND TERESA BELLISSIMO ARE CREDITED WITH INVENTING BUFFALO CHICKEN WINGS AT THE ANCHOR BAR IN BUFFALO, NEW YORK.

½ cup mayonnaise

¼ cup plain yogurt

2 oz crumbled blue cheese (½ cup)

4 celery ribs, cut into thin sticks

3 lb chicken wings (12 to 14)

2 tablespoons vegetable oil (if grilling) or 6 cups vegetable oil (if deep-frying)

½ stick (¼ cup) unsalted butter

3 to 4 tablespoons hot sauce

1½ tablespoons cider vinegar

Whisk together mayonnaise and yogurt in a bowl, then stir in blue cheese (dressing will not be smooth).

Soak celery in a bowl of ice and cold water at least 30 minutes and up to 1 hour.

Cut off chicken wing tips and halve wings at joint.

TO GRILL WINGS:

Prepare grill for cooking.

Pat wings dry. Rub 2 tablespoons oil onto wings and season with salt. Grill on an oiled rack set 5 to 6 inches over glowing coals until cooked through and golden brown, 8 to 10 minutes on each side.

TO DEEP-FRY WINGS:

Heat 6 cups oil in a 5- to 6-quart deep heavy pot until a deep-fat thermometer registers 380°F. Just before oil reaches 380°F, pat dry 6 or 7 wings. Carefully lower wings into oil and fry, stirring occasionally, until cooked through and golden and crisp, 5 to 8 minutes. Transfer with a slotted spoon to paper towels to drain. Pat dry and fry remaining wings in same manner, returning oil to 380°F between batches.

Melt butter in a large skillet over moderately low heat, then stir in hot sauce, vinegar, and salt to taste. Add grilled or fried wings and toss to coat.

Serve wings warm or room temperature with dressing and celery sticks.

COOKS' NOTES

• Dressing may be made 8 hours ahead and chilled, covered.

• We used Frank's Hot Sauce (available at most supermarkets), the original ingredient in these wings. However, it wasn't quite spicy enough on its own for our taste so we added a little Tabasco to increase the heat.

SERVES 6

Pickled black-eyed peas

1 cup dried black-eyed peas

1 yellow bell pepper, cut into ¼-inch dice

½ red bell pepper, cut into ¼-inch dice

½ fresh jalapeño chile, seeded and minced

¼ cup extra-virgin olive oil

¼ cup white-wine vinegar

¼ cup minced fresh chives

2 tablespoons minced red onion

1 teaspoon minced garlic

Accompaniment: toasts

Pick over peas and cover with cold water by 2 inches in a saucepan. Bring water to a boil and boil peas 2 minutes. Remove from heat and soak peas 1 hour. Drain in a sieve.

Simmer peas in water to cover in a saucepan until tender, about 20 minutes, then drain in a sieve.

Stir together peas with all remaining ingredients and salt and pepper to taste. Chill, covered, 4 hours. Serve peas chilled or at room temperature.

COOKS' NOTE

• Pickled peas can be made 2 days ahead and chilled, covered.

SERVES 6

Toasted-nut shortbread

1 stick (½ cup) unsalted butter, softened

¼ cup superfine granulated sugar

½ teaspoon vanilla

⅛ teaspoon salt

1 cup all-purpose flour

½ cup chopped toasted nuts, such as pecans, hazelnuts, or almonds

Preheat oven to 375°F.

Blend together butter, sugar, vanilla, and salt in a bowl with a fork. Sift in flour and blend with fork until mixture forms a soft dough. Transfer to an ungreased large baking sheet, then pat into a 9-by 4½-inch rectangle. Crimp edges decoratively and prick dough all over with fork. Score dough crosswise with the back of a knife into 8 sections. Sprinkle with nuts and press gently into dough with your fingertips.

Bake in middle of oven until edges are golden, about 15 minutes. Cool shortbread on baking sheet on a rack 10 minutes, then cut into slices with a sharp knife while still warm. Transfer slices with a spatula to rack to cool completely.

COOKS' NOTE

• We topped our shortbread with toasted nuts, but it's just as delicious on its own.

MAKES 8 COOKIES

Page numbers in **bold** indicate photographs.

Chocolate, Giant, 125
Coconut, Toasted-, 58, **59**
Meringue Kisses, 106, **107**
Pistachio Brown-Sugar, 32
Shortbread, Toasted-Nut, **185**, 185

CORNMEAL Pancakes, Cream Cheese, with Dried
Cranberries and Apricots in Maple Syrup,
82, 82

CORN
Chicken and Sausage Maque Choux, 57
Creamy, with Chives, **66**, 66
Grilled, with Cayenne Butter, 149
and Pork Kebabs with Rosemary Green Beans
and Potatoes, **152**, 152
and Tomato "Nachos" with Spicy Guacamole, 151

CORN BREAD, 118
Chicken, Pulled Barbecued, on, 118

CRAB Melts, 117

CRACKERS, Hazelnut, with Stilton and Fresh Figs,
179, 179

CRANBERRY(IES)
Coolers, -Lime, 101
Dried, and Apricots in Maple Syrup, Cornmeal
Cream Cheese Pancakes with, **82**, 82
Toddies, Brandied, 69

CREAM CHEESE
Cheesecake, Three Cities of Spain, **73**, 73
Cornmeal Pancakes, with Dried Cranberries and
Apricots in Maple Syrup, **82**, 82
Frosting, Blossom-Topped Cupcakes, 114, **115**
Onion, Caramelized, and Roasted Red Pepper
Dip, 173
Red Pepper and Arugula Spirals, 139

CRUST(S)
Crumb, 73
Crumb, Cheesecake, Three Cities of Spain, **73**, 73
Gingersnap, Blueberry-Lemon Tartlets with, 157
Shortbread, Raspberry Semifreddo Torte,
150, 153

CUCUMBER(S)
Asparagus, and Sugar Snap Peas with Herb
Garlic Dip, **29**, 30
Caviar Canapés, **100**, 105
Pickled, and Smoked Salmon on Rye, 20
Slaw, Spicy, **116**, 119
Summer Rolls, Vegetable, 169
Watercress Salad, Chopped, with Sesame Seeds
and, 166

CUPCAKES
Blossom-Topped, 114, **115**
edible flower garnish for, 115

CURRANT Tea Scones, **62**, 63

CURRY(IED)
Chicken Liver Pâté, **105**, 105
Peanut Sauce, Chicken Satés with, 18, **19**
Pork Loin, Apricot-Stuffed, 97
Salt, Rib-Eye Steaks with, 47, **48**

CUSTARD
Flan, Cinnamon-Coffee, 93
Semifreddo Torte, Raspberry, **150**, 153

D

DESSERTS. **See also** Bars; Cake(s); Cookies; Fruit
Desserts; Ice Cream; Pie(s)
Flan, Cinnamon-Coffee, 93
Gelées, Grape, with Berries, 33
Granita, Peach-Almond, 160
Semifreddo Torte, Raspberry, **150**, 153
Sorbet, Coconut Lime, 26
Sorbet, Orange Star-Anise, 87
Tartlets, Blueberry-Lemon, with Gingersnap
Crusts, 157
Tiramisù, 79

DESSERT SAUCE(S)
Caramel, Coffee Ice Cream Chocolate Stack
with, 15
Maple Calvados, Broiled Apples with, **49**, 49

DIPPING SAUCE(S)
Garlic, Greek, Shrimp Satés with, 18, **19**
Peanut Curry, Chicken Satés with, 18, **19**
Southeast Asian, Grilled Lobsters with, **146**, 147
for Vegetable Summer Rolls, 169

DIPS AND SPREADS
Chicken Liver Pâté, Curried, **105**, 105
Goat Cheese and Sun-Dried Tomato, Herbed, 47
Guacamole, Spicy, Tomato and Corn "Nachos"
with, 151
Herb Garlic, Asparagus, Cucumbers, and Sugar
Snap Peas with, **29**, 30
Mousse, Piquillo Pepper, with Pita Chips, 96
Onion, Caramelized, and Roasted Red Pepper,
173
Salsa, Peanut-Mango, with Jícama Chips, 117
Salsa Ranchera, **90**, 92
Tapenade, Green Olive and Almond, **20**, 20

Pasta with Tomatoes and, **14**, 14
Spinach, and Bacon Salad with Pecans, 65
and Sun-Dried Tomato Spread, Herbed, 47

H

I

J

S

SABLEFISH, Smoked, Canapés, 96

SAGE, Kabocha Squash Soup, Roasted, with Pancetta and, **84**, 85

SALAD(S). **See also** Slaw
Black-Eyed Pea, 118
Bread-and-Tomato, Lebanese (Fatoosh), **31**, 31
Fennel and Romaine, with Marinated Roasted Peppers, 130
Greek Country, **75**, 75
Greens, Baby, with Apple-Maple Vinaigrette, 180
Napa Cabbage, Asian Pear, and Carrot, 49
Noodle, Crunchy, with Orange-Sesame Dressing, 124
Orange, Jícama, and Cilantro, 26
Orzo, Pine Nut, and Feta, 32
Pear, Pine Nut and Watercress, 87
Potato, Garlic, and Red Pepper, Roasted, 140, **141**
Radicchio and Boston Lettuce with Garlic Vinaigrette, 37
Red-Leaf Lettuce with Shallot Vinaigrette, **153**, 155
Rice, with Peas and Mint, 175
Romaine, Parsley, and Fennel, with Tapenade Vinaigrette, 70
Spinach, Baby, and Mint, **98**, 98
Spinach, Bacon, and Goat Cheese, with Pecans, 65
Spinach, Red Pepper, and Mango, Grilled Squid on, 160, **161**
Sweet-Potato, Grilled, 140, **141**
Tomatoes with Green Goddess Dressing, 66
Vegetable, Grilled, Cold Roast Beef Tenderloin with, 65
Wild Rice, **7**, 110
Yellow Squash, Grilled, and Orzo, 156

SALAD DRESSING. **See also** Vinaigrette
Blue Cheese, for Buffalo Wings, **182**, 184
Green Goddess, Tomatoes with, 66
Orange-Sesame, Crunchy Noodle Salad with, 124

SALMON, Smoked, and Pickled Cucumber on Rye, 20

SALSA
Avocado and Roasted Tomatillo, Grilled Shrimp with, **23**, 23
Peanut-Mango, with Jícama Chips, 117
Ranchera, **90**, 92

Tomato-Olive, Grilled Polenta Cakes with, 159

SALT, Curried, Rib-Eye Steaks with, 47, **48**

SANDWICHES
Chicken, Sesame, with Napa Cabbage and Spinach Slaw on Baguette, **170**, 170
Lobster Salad, Minted, in Pitas, **168**, 171
Tuna and Olive Salad, **166**, 166

SATÉS
Chicken with Peanut Curry Sauce, 18, **19**
Shrimp, with Greek Garlic Sauce, 18, **19**

SAUCE(S). **See also** Dipping Sauce(s); Salsa
Garlic, Green Beans in, 169
Gravy, Pan, Lamb, Leg of, Green Olive, Lemon, and Garlic-Roasted, with Potatoes and, 128, **129**
Pizza, 79
Pumpkin Seed, Roasted Red Snapper Fillets with, 25
Tomato-Onion Jus, Veal Shanks, Braised, with Mashed Potatoes and, **71**, 71

SAUSAGE and Chicken Maque Choux, **57**, 57

SCALLOPS, Grilled, with Tomato-Onion Relish, 127

SCONES, Currant Tea, **62**, 63

SESAME (SEEDS)
Chicken with Napa Cabbage and Spinach Slaw on Baguette, **170**, 170
Noodle Salad, Asian, 145
-Orange Dressing, Crunchy Noodle Salad with, 124
Watercress Salad, Chopped, with Cucumber and, 166

SHALLOT(S)
Crunch Mix, Spicy, 165
Vinaigrette, Red-Leaf Lettuce with, 155

SHELLFISH. **See also** Shrimp
Crab Melts, 117
Lobsters, Grilled, with Southeast Asian Dipping Sauce, **146**, 147
Lobster Salad, Minted, in Pitas, **168**, 171
Scallops, Grilled, with Tomato-Onion Relish, 127

SHERRY, Spiced, 101

SHORTBREAD
Base for Bars, 176
Toasted-Nut, **185**, 185

SHRIMP
Grilled, with Avocado and Roasted Tomatillo Salsa, **23**, 23

Any items in the photographs not credited are privately owned.

FRONT JACKET: See credits below for "Frontispiece."

BACK JACKET: Stainless-steel table—Williams-Sonoma, (800) 541-2233 or williams-sonoma.com. Conical salad bowl, rectangular and oval white platters, wine glasses and napkin—Crate & Barrel, (800) 996-9960.

FRONTMATTER

Caipirinhas (page 1): See credits below for "Fresh from the Sea Grill."

Frontispiece (page 2): Cucina Fresca "Saffron" dinner plates and salad bowls; "Foglia" footed bread and butter plates—Vietri, (800) 277-5933. Tulip wine clear bubble glasses—Mariposa, (800) 788-1304. "Dark" French stainless flatware—Smith & Hawken, (800) 940-1170.

Outdoor table setting (page 5): See credits below for "Graduation Day Party."

Curried Chicken Liver Pâté (page 6, top): See credits below for "Oscar Night Party."

Table setting (page 8): See credits below for "Dinner on the Porch."

Easy Saturday Nights

DINNER ON THE PORCH

People drinking wine on porch (page 12): Wineglasses—Williams-Sonoma, (800) 541-2233.

Table setting (page 15): "Edme" Wedgewood earthenware plates—for stores call (800) 955-1550. Sterling knives and forks, London 1792–1807—F. Gorevic & Son, (212) 753-9319. "Burgundy" crystal wineglasses from the Oenology Collection—Baccarat, (212) 826-4100. "Tabriz" linen place mats—Ad Hoc Softwares, (212) 925-2652. Rushed urn—Briger Design, (212) 517-4489.

COME FOR COCKTAILS

Lantern on fence post (page 17): Coach lantern—for stores call Design Ideas, (800) 426-6394. Photographed at the vineyards and fruit farm of Mr. Sam Argetsinger in the Finger Lakes Region, New York.

Chicken Satés with Peanut Curry Sauce; Shrimp Satés with Greek Garlic Sauce (page 19): Coconut shell bowls—for stores contact The Global Table, (212) 979-7574.

MEXICAN DINNER

Table setting (pages 22 and 26): "Rope" ceramic service plates, footed tin bowl (centerpiece), and candles—Bloomingdale's, (800) 555-7467. Dinner plates, napkins, and table runner—Pan American Phoenix, (212) 570-0300. "Stonehenge" flatware and green striped glasses—Pottery Barn, (800) 840-2843. Tables, chairs, bench, and pillows—Jamson Whyte, (305) 535-2224.

Grilled Shrimp with Avocado and Roasted Tomatillo Salsa (page 23): "Flore" crystal compote—Baccarat, (212) 826-4100.

Buffet setting (page 29): "Capri" white ceramic bowls; "Crackle" blue ceramic bowls; "Lido" blue tumblers and blue double Old Fashioned glasses—Pottery Barn, (800) 922-5507. "Splash" blue glasses (on counter)—for stores, call Izabel Lam, (718) 797-3983. "Beach" linen napkins—ABH Design, (212) 688-3764.

DINNER BY THE FIRE

Hot Cider with Rum; Honey-Roasted Peppered Pecans (page 39): Crackle bowl (with nuts)—Daniel Levy, (212) 268-0878. Cider glasses—Ad Hoc Softwares, (888) 748-4852.

Lemon Molasses Chess Pie (page 43): Plastic-handled stainless-steel flatware by Dubost—Sur La Table, (800) 243-0852. Cotton napkin by Shyam Ahuja—Simon Pearce, (212) 421-8801.

LAST-MINUTE DINNER

Edamame (page 47): "Yoshino" square crystal plates—The Hoya Crystal Gallery, (212) 223-6335.

Lazy Sundays

BEACH HOUSE BRUNCH

Cups and saucers and flatware (page 52): "Kristy" earthenware cups and saucers; "New Kings" sterling flatware; "Cottage Lane Floral" cotton napkin (beneath)—The Ralph Lauren Home Collection, (212) 642-8700.

Honeydew Mimosas (page 53): "Edward Continental Champagne" flute (left) and "Landon Continental Champagne" flute (right)—The Ralph Lauren Home Collection, (212) 642-8700.

Baked Eggs in Brioches (page 54): Plate—Ad Hoc Softwares, (888) 748-4852. Cup and saucer—Fishs Eddy, (877) 347-4733.

CAJUN COMFORTS

Brown-Sugar Pecan Ice Cream; Toasted Coconut Cookies (page 59): Hand-thrown and hand-glazed earthenware bowls—for stores call Potluck Studios, (914) 626-2300.

DROP BY FOR COFFEE

Woman reading newspaper on porch (page 61): Photographed at Blackberry Farm (formerly the Inn at Blackberry Farm), 1471 West Millers Cove Road, Walland, TN 37886, (865) 380-2260.

Currant Scones (page 62): "Luna" porcelain cups, saucers, and dessert plates—Calvin Klein, for store locations call (800) 294-7978. Coffee pot, creamer, and jam pots—Takashimaya, (212) 350-0100. Linen napkin—Frank McIntosh Home Collection at Henri Bendel, (212) 247-1100.

Woman reading on sofa (page 63): Clothing—Anthropologie, (800) 309-2500. Cup and saucer—Nicole Farhi, (212) 223-8811.

SNOWBOUND SUNDAY

Table setting (page 68): Green throw (on sofa)—ABH Design, (212) 688-3764. Wineglasses—Villeroy & Boch, (800) 845-5376. Striped cashmere and wool blanket with fringe (on table)—Meg Cohen, (212) 473-4002.

Braised Veal Shanks with Mashed Potatoes and Tomato Onion Jus (page 71): "Geranium" stoneware dinner plate—Fioriware, (740) 454-7400, ext. 21.

FIRESIDE PIZZA
Prosciutto and Arugula Pizza; Pizza with Garlic and Olive Oil (page 77): "Antica Roma" and "Atene" majolica dinner plates—for stores call Deruta of Italy, (212) 686-0808. Carafe and glasses—Zabar's, (212) 787-2000 or (800) 697-6301. Wood-burning oven—Mugnaini Imports, (888) 887-7206.

LASAGNE SUPPER
Tomato and Mozzarella Lasagne (page 86): Marble bowl—Tuscan Square, (212) 977-7777. Fringed napkins—Material Possessions, (312) 280-4885.

Easy Celebrations

A SMALL ENGAGEMENT PARTY
Mi Rosa; Champagne Cocktail (page 95): "Epoque" flute by Kosta Boda, (212) 752-1095.

OSCAR NIGHT PARTY
Cucumber Caviar Canapés (page 100): Eighteenth-century glass pâté dish (sour cream); glass tazza (caviar; one of four), circa 1910—James II Galleries, (212) 355-7040. "Perfection" crystal Martini glasses—Baccarat, (212) 826-4100.

Mustard-Seed Cheddar Sticks (page 101): "Perfection" crystal Martini glasses—Baccarat, (212) 826-4100.

Curried Chicken Liver Pâté (page 105): Wineglasses; square dish; stone-colored napkins—Banana Republic, (888) 277-8953. Stoneware vase—Jonathan Adler, (212) 941-8950. Footed stone—Bed, Bath & Beyond, (800) GOBEYOND.

Meringue Kisses; Lemon Curd (page 107): Sterling compote (lemon curd)—S. Wyler, (212) 879-9848.

COME MEET THE BABY
Sparkling Strawberry Mint Lemonade (page 109): "Calistoga" etched glasses—Crate & Barrel, (800) 996-9960.

Herb-Roasted Turkey Breast; Sautéed Sugar Snap Peas (page 113): Conical salad bowl and tulip linen tablecloth—Crate & Barrel, (800) 996-9960. White linen napkins courtesy of ABC Carpet & Home, (212) 473-3000. Belle Provence "Azure Blue" oval platter and small serving bowl and "Whitewashed" dinner plate—Mariposa, (800) 788-1304.

GRADUATION DAY PARTY
Spicy Slaw (page 116): Horn servers—Ad Hoc Softwares, (212) 925-2652.

Outdoor Table Setting (page 120): "Canyon Road" white earthenware dinner plates; "Grafton Stripe" cotton blanket—The Ralph Lauren Home Collection, (212) 642-8700. Tin dinner plates and mugs—Pottery Barn, (800) 922-5507. Vintage wineglasses; glass mugs; nineteenth-century spongeware bowl—Pantry & Hearth, (212) 532-0535. Wood-handled flatware—Ad Hoc Softwares, (212) 925-2652. "Original Mug" metal mugs—for stores call Wilton Armetale, (800) 826-0088. Blue-and-white striped linen napkins—Mecox Gardens, (516) 287-5015. Russian embroidered napkins—Françoise Nunnallé,

(212) 246-4281. Late-nineteenth-century sterling napkin rings—More & More, (212) 580-8404. Red and blue pillow; red and white pillow—ABH Design, (212) 688-3764. Denim pillows—Crate & Barrel, (800) 996-9960. Yellow sap bucket; "Fat Lady" pine table with painted base by El Paso; hickory high chair, circa 1930—Zona, (212) 925-6750, ext. 15. Late-eighteenth-century fruitwood bench; hickory armchairs, circa 1910—Newel Art Galleries, (212) 758-1970.

A POOL PARTY FOR THE KIDS

Pool and patio (page 122): Photographed on location at Hope Springs Resort, Desert Hot Springs, CA—(760) 329-4003.

Easy Grills

Table setting (page 136): See credits below for "Lobster on the Grill."

STEAK ON THE GRILL

Man at grill (page 138): Photographed on location at Hope Springs Resort, Desert Hot Springs, CA—(760) 329-4003. Weber Kettle Grill—Gracious Home, (212) 517-6300. Man's Shirt—Paul Smith, (212) 627-9773.

Roasted Potato, Garlic, and Red Pepper Salad; Grilled Sweet-Potato Salad (page 141): Hand-blown glass bowls—Church and Maple Glass Studio, Burlington, VT, (802) 863-3880.

LOBSTER ON THE GRILL

Lobster with Southeast Asian Dipping Sauce and table setting (page 146): Aqua glass plates by Fossilglass—First Cup, (617) 244-4468. "Williams Collection" wineglasses—Williams-Sonoma, (800) 541-1262. Raffia-wrapped pitchers (with flowers); hurricane lamps—Ad Hoc Softwares, (212) 925-2652. Linen napkins—Simon Pearce, (800) 774-5277. Shell napkin rings—Tommy Bahama, (941) 643-7920. Candleholders (on railing)—Anthropologie, (212) 343-7070.

PORK ON THE GRILL

Corn and Pork Kebabs with Rosemary Green Beans and Potatoes (page 152): Blue-and-white "Gingham" dinner plate; white salad plate—Crate & Barrel, (800) 996-9960.

CHICKEN ON THE GRILL

People eating salad (page 154): White dinner plates by Syracuse—Bloomingdale's, (212) 705-2000.

Grilled Lemon-Herb Marinated Chicken (page 155): "Trifid" hand-forged sterling knife and forks; "Round English" hand-forged sterling knife and fork—James Robinson, (212) 752-6166.

FRESH FROM THE SEA GRILL

Caipirinhas (page 159): Stainless-steel pitcher—Bridge Kitchenware, (212) 688-4220. "Balance" Old Fashioned glasses—Pottery Barn, (800) 922-5507.

Grilled Shrimp on Spinach, Red Pepper, and Mango Salad (page 161, lower): Carafe—Algabar, (310) 360-3500. "Magnum" stainless fork—OK, (323) 653-3501. Chair—Smith & Hawken, (310) 247-0737.

Easy Picnics

PICNIC AT THE BEACH

Picnic setting (page 164): Nineteenth-century pine trunk—Wayne Pratt, Inc., (508) 228-8788. "Chaîne d'Ancre" porcelain plates; "Attelage" stainless-steel flatware; Wicker grooming basket—Hermès, (800) 441-4488. Beach towels—for stores call The Ralph Lauren Home Collection, (212) 642-8700. White cotton piqué napkins—Bergdorf Goodman, (800) 218-4918. Brass lamp; spyglass; signal flags; rope (around napkin)—E & B Marine Catalog, (800) 262-8464.

LUNCHBOX PICNIC

Minted Lobster Salad in Pita (page 168) and Sesame Chicken with Napa Cabbage and Spinach Slaw on Baguette (page 170): Stainless-steel lunch boxes—Ad Hoc Softwares, (212) 925-2652.

PICNIC AT THE LAKE

Canoe at dock (page 174): Bandanas (covering pillows)—Outdoor Traders, (203) 862-9696. Wool blanket—Ad Hoc Softwares, (212) 925-2652. Red-and-white striped cotton rug—Crate & Barrel, (800) 996-9960.

APPLE ORCHARD PICNIC

Picking apples (page 178): photographed at Breezy Hill Orchard, 828 Centre Road, Staatsburg, NY, (914) 266-3979.

Hazelnut Crackers with Stilton and Fresh Figs (page 179): Colorstone plate by Sasaki—for stores call (212) 686-5080.

We gratefully acknowledge ROMULO A. YANES, Gourmet photographer, for the majority of photographs that appear in this book. We also acknowledge the photographers listed below whose work was previously published in Gourmet magazine.

MELANIE ACEVEDO: Wild Rice Salad (page 7, center); Tomato and Mozzarella Lasagne (page 86); Curried Chicken Liver Pâté (pages 6, upper, and 105); Lake scene (page 172).

QUENTIN BACON: Pasta with Tomatoes and Goat Cheese (pages 6, lower, and 14); Martini (page 16); Fattoosh (page 31); Hot Cider with Rum and Honey-Roasted Peppered Pecans (page 39); Woman with dog (page 68); Snow scene (page 69); Boys jumping into pool (page 124).

ANTOINE BOOTZ: Woman standing at pantry (page 46).

JEAN CAZALS: Assorted cheeses (page 45).

MIKI DUISTERHOF: Woman reading on sofa (page 63, detail on page 60); White four-poster bed (page 80); Spicy Slaw (page 116).

DANA GALLAGHER: Farmstand (page 34).

LISA HUBBARD: Glass of red wine (page 126).

ELISABETH HUGHES: Blueberries on a plate (page 157).

JOHN KERNICK: Picking apples (page 178).

RICK LEW: Boats in harbor (page 158).

RITA MAAS: Creamy Corn with Chives (page 66).

MAURA MCEVOY: Buffet setting (page 111).

MINH + WASS: Bicycle at the Beach (page 162); Fence at the Beach (page 167).

VICTORIA PEARSON: Grilled Shrimp on Spinach, Red Pepper, and Mango Salad (page 161).

DAN PEEBLES: Swimming pool and patio (page 122); Man grilling steaks (page 138).

NICK POPE: Mixing bowl with batter (page 81).

ALAN RICHARDSON: Broiled Apples with Maple Calvados Sauce (page 49); Baked Eggs in Brioche (page 54); Herbs in tin cup (page 56); Chicken and Sausage Maque Choux (page 57); Strawberry-Rhubarb Parfaits (page 149).

ELLEN SILVERMAN: Woman reading paper on porch (page 61).

JONELLE WEAVER: Silverware on napkin (page 108).

ANNA WILLIAMS: Three Cities of Spain Cheesecake (page 73); Golden Cake with Chocolate Sour Cream Frosting (page 133).

Grateful acknowledgment is made to the following contributors for permission to reprint recipes previously published in Gourmet magazine:

FOUR SEASONS HOTEL, ATLANTA, GA: Sparkling Strawberry Mint Lemonade (page 109). Copyright © 1999.

LOUIS OSTEEN: Spicy Slaw (page 119). Copyright © 2000.

MARIA DE LOS ANGELES RODRIGUEZ ARTACHO: Tortilla Española (page 180). Copyright © 2000.

MICHELE AND CHARLES SCICOLONE: Pizza with Garlic and Olive Oil (page 76). Copyright © 1998. Prosciutto and Arugula Pizza (page 78). Copyright© 1998.

ZANNE EARLY STEWART: Pommes Anna (page 40). Copyright © 1995.

MARK STRAUSMAN: Grilled Lemon-Herb Marinated Chicken (page 155). Copyright © 1998.

MEASURE LIQUIDS in glass or clear plastic liquid-measuring cups and **dry ingredients** in nesting dry-measuring cups (usually made of metal or plastic) that can be leveled off with a knife.

MEASURE FLOUR by spooning (not scooping) it into a dry-measuring cup and leveling off with a knife without tapping or shaking cup.

DO NOT SIFT FLOUR unless specified in recipe. If sifted flour is called for, sift flour before measuring. (Many brands say "presifted" on the label: disregard this.)

WHEN WE CALL FOR A SHALLOW BAKING PAN, we mean an old-fashioned jelly-roll or four-sided cookie pan.

MEASURE SKILLETS AND BAKING PANS across the top, not the bottom.

TO PREPARE A WATER BATH for baking, put your filled pan in a larger pan and add enough boiling-hot water to reach halfway up the side of the smaller pan.

USE LIGHT-COLORED METAL PANS for baking unless otherwise specified. If using dark metal pans, including nonstick, your baked goods will likely brown more and the cooking times may be shorter.

WASH AND DRY ALL PRODUCE before using.

BEFORE PREPPING FRESH HERBS OR GREENS, remove the leaves or fronds from the stems—the exception is cilantro, which has tender stems. Pack fresh herbs or greens before measuring.

BLACK PEPPER in recipes is always freshly ground.

WEAR PROTECTIVE GLOVES when handling **chiles**.

GRATE CHEESES just before using.

TO ZEST CITRUS FRUITS, remove the colored part of the rind only (avoid the bitter white pith). For strips, use a vegetable peeler. For grated zest, use the smallest teardrop-shaped holes or the tiny sharp ones on a four-sided grater.

TOAST SPICES in a dry heavy skillet over moderate heat, stirring, until fragrant and a shade or two darker. **Toast nuts** in a shallow baking pan in a 350° F oven until golden, 5 to 10 minutes. **Toast seeds** either way.

TO PEEL A TOMATO OR PEACH, first cut an × in the end opposite the stem and immerse in boiling water (10 seconds for a tomato or 15 seconds for a peach). Transfer it to ice water and then peel.